UNLEASH POSSIBLE

A MARKETING PLAYBOOK THAT DRIVES B2B SALES

Published with Stress Free Publishers by Samantha Stone

www.unleashpossible.com

Edited by: Katie Martell

Cover Design by: Dan Greenwald

ISBN 13: 978-1-937985-88-2
ISBN 10: 1-937985-88-1

Printed in the U.S.A.

Unleash Possible is a registered trademark of The Marketing Advisory Network.

The information in this book includes case studies and provides advice based on the author's observations, industry research and her own experiences. While it is the author's hope that the content will inspire you to apply what's learned, it is recognized that every company and every buyer community is different. Your business should always conduct your own due diligence prior to following any guidance in this book to ensure new programs or changes to the organization are well suited to your company's culture and business goals. You alone are responsible for the consequences of using the tools and lessons within.

PRAISE FOR *UNLEASH POSSIBLE*

"This is a book that should not only be read by marketers. It's a book that should be *on the desk of every executive in the company*. It should be required reading for the head of sales, technology, and most importantly, the CEO, to help create a shared vision of marketing to grow and sustain the business (and to do it well!)" *Jere Doyle, Managing Director Sigma Prime Ventures*

"*Unleash Possible* is filled with case studies and practical "how-tos" delivered with Samantha's warmth and unique insight. It lends a clear path for how to progress your organization forward. She not only shares what we should, and should not, be doing, but she shows you how to get it done, and how to hold marketing accountable to meaningful business metrics." Claudine Bianchi CMO, ClickSoftware

"Rarely do you find a practical, accessible resource that seamlessly combines sales and marketing into a coherent and motivating call to action as Samantha has written here. Highly recommended read by those new (and old) to B2B sales and marketing (yes both sides of the aisle and funnel!)." Matt Heinz, President Heinz Marketing Inc.

"*Unleash Possible is a shot in the arm for any marketer (or sales person) who is needing guidance and support. The pages are that of a coach who is encouraging their team that the seemingly impossible is indeed achievable. Marketing executives should add this book to their teams reading list as not only does it encourage teams to get up and get going, it provides practical advice and insights that can implemented immediately.*" Carlos Hidalgo CEO ANNUITAS & Author of *"Driving Demand"*

"*The most realistic assessment of what's going on in B2B marketing today that I've seen. I love the practical, actionable slant, and the case studies that are used to illustrate the story.*" Anne Janzer, Marketer and Author

"*Unleash Possible* is a no-nonsense book with **actionable** advice that marketers can use to realize their company›s potential. Samantha does this leveraging her straight-forward manner, citing her own real-life experiences to illustrate not just what to do, but how to do it. Easy to read and entertaining to boot, Unleash Possible is a must read for any marketer looking to honestly evaluate their marketing plan and hinge it to what›s important to their company." Maribeth Ross, CMO Monetate

"The author's acute awareness of her own learning brings valuable gifts forward in her book. Accepting these gifts and absorbing her ideas will fast-track your success." Peter Bauer, CEO Mimecast

"I first had the privilege of working with Samantha nearly 20 years ago, when I watched her build one of the most dominant Channels Marketing organizations in the document management software space. Since then, I have considered her a trusted advisor in helping me to develop marketing, lead generation, and sales-driving strategies within retail organizations ranging in size from start-ups to $70B/yr in revenue. Samantha is fantastic at helping business leaders explore innovative solutions with a smart balance of creativity, pragmatism, and insight. Unleash Possible delivers the same fantastic best practices that I have seen drive success for her companies and clients." Jamie Dooley, Retail eCommerce Executive

"Unleash Possible helps you create the necessary (but often elusive) connection between product, sales, and marketing." Ann Handley, Chief Content Officer, MarketingProfs

TABLE OF CONTENTS

An investor, a CEO and a CMO walk into a boardroom…

FOREWORD

Jere Doyle,
Managing Director at Sigma Prime Ventures

Every business is presented with a simple choice: prioritize marketing, or fail.

Marketing has changed significantly. It's true there are far more marketing methods, channels, tools and opportunities to reach our audience than ever before. Yet, one important thing never changes: marketing still is, and always has been, about acquiring customers at the right cost, and keeping those customers.

What *has* changed is the role marketing plays in a business. As an investor and advisor to many businesses, I often find marketing to be an afterthought. This is a critical mistake in today's environment. If you build it, they will not come. In fact, they will quickly find another option.

Companies that are successful have done the work to put a strong marketing strategy in place. They know that sales and growth don't happen by accident, or without the right customer acquisition strategy in place, early on.

Successful business leaders know they must make the choice to master marketing in an age when buyers expect each vendor to know them, inside and out; to be prepared with content that stands out and that allows buyers to self-educate; and to provide a buying experience that is tailor-made for their problems, their vertical, and their expectations.

That's why, when I read *Unleash Possible* I was so bolstered by what it has to say. This is a book that should not only be read by marketers—it should be *on the desk of every executive in the company.* It should be required reading for the head of sales, head of technology, and most important, the CEO—to help create a shared vision of marketing to grow and sustain the business. (And to do it well!)

As Samantha points out early in the book, culture matters. A great marketing culture begins at the top, with the CEO. The CEO sets the tone and priorities of the organization, builds a structure of support and makes choices that dictate the path for the rest of your team. And today, CEOs are faced with that simple choice: invest in and prioritize marketing, or fail. This can no longer be an afterthought.

If I have learned anything, it is that success in this world happens as a result of series of right choices. When you read this book, you'll see not only how important marketing is to the success of your business, but also the choices you need to make to get it right.

Peter Bauer

CEO & Cofounder, Mimecast

A company's CEO has to sell possibilities: a future that may be unleashed in their own mind but has not yet formed for others. The more meaningful and vivid these possibilities, the more the leader can attract teammates, customers, investors and followers. This is a job the CEO cannot do alone. A successful movement always needs others to believe upfront, to build the momentum needed to begin, and to sustain energy to see the vision through to execution. Leadership is an age-old skill and marketing is fundamentally a leadership craft. Marketing must always start with the question "Who are we trying to reach?" Followed by "Why do they need to pay attention?"

Once the vision is articulated, what comes next is even harder; turning the promised possibilities into experienced realities. We must now more fully unleash what has been sold as possible by building and doing. This is a longer game and one that cannot be done without marketing.

Unleash Possible takes us on an adventure from Samantha's journey as a young woman selling door-to-door, through to her experiences as a marketing leader at several successful technology companies. What strikes me is how much we can understand about our own businesses from her deep consciousness and awareness of her learning as a marketer while she worked to make some intriguing possibilities into realities. Her acute awareness of her own learning brings valuable gifts forward in her book. Accepting these gifts and absorbing her ideas will fast-track your success.

If you are a student wondering what it's like to work in marketing, this book will tell you. It's a lens showing marketing in action, with an invitation to every meeting and an eye on every campaign. Don't be surprised if you feel an extraordinary readiness for the real world of work after you have read it.

If you are a marketing veteran or a business leader, this book will take you back to first principles and then show you the way through common missteps. It will reconnect you with the fun and value of raw creativity. But perhaps most important, as a leader in business, it will connect you with insight into the experience of smart people working in your marketing organization. It will remind you of what is important to them, how they can be more effective and how you can use marketing to lead more effectively.

Although marketing is part of a greater whole, it has an unquestionable leadership obligation. This book invites you and your entire team to connect with conviction and clarity, both to challenge assumptions and grab hold of opportunity—to unleash possible in new and exciting ways.

By Claudine Bianchi
CMO, ClickSoftware

Wake up, marketers! Buyers are changing every day and we will fail if we don't keep up with them. It starts by measuring marketing against the right things—business outcomes.

It has never been more important for all of us to be continually evaluating our marketing programs. Long gone are the days when you developed an annual plan with everything buttoned up and the only question your CEO or CFO asked was "What are we really getting for this huge marketing spend?" It's always huge to people not in marketing.

Marketing deserves a seat at the boardroom table—driving the business, not simply serving it. But to do so we need to make these three constants a part of our core:

- o Know our customers
- o Align with sales
- o Measure, analyze, evaluate constantly—then be agile and act on what we learn

Over the past decade, the dominance of digital marketing allows us to measure the effectiveness of our marketing efforts as never before. We can now track when a prospect visits our website, following along and guiding them through their buyers' journey to when they become customers and even advocates.

With this backdrop, we need to get much better at learning about our customers—the emergence of personas has revolutionized the way we segment and communicate to our constituents. The combination of qualitative and quantitative data gives us much more than demographic profiles. Now, with psychographics, we can discover what motivates our potential customers and what triggers them to buy.

Gaining these insights, marketing is no longer just the brochure makers and "branding" people—we are true partners with sales, driving not just outputs, but outcomes; not just leads, but opportunities. More and more, we are measured the same way as our sales counterparts—on pipeline growth and revenue.

This is an important shift, and for many it is scary. Marketing has been given a seat at the table, but we've been measured differently from everyone else—by top-of-the-funnel metrics like MQLs, not real outcomes like closed business. Executive teams are beginning to acknowledge marketing's contribution to growth and the integral role we play in building the relationship with customers. Now is the most opportune time to align ourselves with the business goals of the CEO, to demonstrate concrete value and to drive overall corporate strategy.

Is this the "Age of the Marketer?"[1] I believe it is.

I've personally always believed that the best strategies are useless unless we can execute against them. It comes down to pragmatic thinking combined with fearless creativity—balancing the right brain and the left brain, rolling up our sleeves, and making things

---

1 https://blog.adroll.com/trends/ashu-garg-foundation-capital-martech-report

happen. What I found so compelling about *Unleash Possible* is that it's practical advice combined with innovative ideas that work.

I've worked with Samantha at numerous companies and have always been energized by her guidance, experience and humor. This book captures the many important lessons that Samantha has learned at both very large and very small companies (and many in-betweens). *Unleash Possible* is filled with case studies and practical how-tos delivered with Samantha's warmth and unique insight. It shows a clear path for how to propel your organization forward. She not only shares what we should, and should not, be doing, she shows you how to get it done—and how to hold marketing accountable to meaningful business metrics.

Whether you are early in your career or a seasoned veteran, you will find value in this book. And, I hope, unleash your possible, too.

INTRODUCTION

I really never meant to be a marketer.

However, judging from my career to date, the universe had other plans. In my career I have delivered over 150,000 marketing-qualified leads, generated more than $500 million in revenue, won 12 distinguished product awards, and had a lot of fun doing it.

My journey has taken me through great success (and great learning moments) at high-growth technology organizations including SAP, Ardent Software (acquired by Informix and ultimately IBM), Maven Networks (acquired by Yahoo!), Mimecast, Axceler (acquired by Metalogix), Netezza (which ultimately had an IPO, then eventually was acquired by IBM), and Dataupia.

All of the above point toward one inevitable truth: I found my passion even if it was by mistake. My destiny as a high growth marketer was sealed before I even knew marketing was more than billboards and annoying television commercials.

After spending my formative years exploring and residing in Connecticut, Greece, Liberia and Singapore, at 17 I settled at a small liberal arts college. At school I studied the closest degree they had to business—economics, with a minor in formal organizations, whatever that meant. I studied hard, and I played even harder.

I worked at the writing center turning half-baked thesis statements into coherent arguments, and in the library checking out my fellow students as they checked out books (yes, I'm experienced enough to remember checking out actual books) to pay for all that playing. At the time I thought these part-time jobs were just about earning spending money without leaving campus. In fact, it was the first sign the universe wanted me to be a marketer.

In hindsight, it would become the foundation for a career of content development and strategy that differentiated offerings, told stories, and inspired action for clients including The Weather Company (an IBM business), Percussion Software and Meridium. Dozens of research studies, hundreds of case studies and too many presentations to count prove it was time well spent.

When I was 22, fresh out of college, I wanted to move to Massachusetts, so I did. But I had no job, and according to the dozen interviews I went on, no hirable skills. Forced by the reality of paying bills, I settled for the highly coveted career of pushing restaurant coupons door-to-door. Each day I was dropped off in a strange neighborhood with a book of "buy one, get one" meal coupons for a nearby restaurant. My goal was to sell as many of these $20 coupon books as I could by knocking on unsuspecting neighborhood doors and offering a smile and a "highly desirable deal" for a restaurant I had never tried, nor knew anything about. This was long before the days of Groupon deals and I was met with a wide range of emotions—skepticism, annoyance, and on a good day, the occasional excitement. As you might imagine, the job was only slightly better than the alternative of dragging around vacuum cleaners door-to-door. The position was 100% commission-based. If I had a good day, I went grocery shopping. If I had a bad day, I ate whatever was cheapest at McDonalds.

After a couple of weeks knocking on doors I started to see patterns: neighborhoods where I'd make a lot of money, and ones where I'd make almost nothing.

Looking for early adopters is a lesson I was eager to apply when we launched Netezza (later IPO and acquired by IBM) and Dataupia to market in highly competitive environments. Securing a company's first 10 customers takes an almost irrational belief in yourself that requires hunger, passion and relentless pursuit of what's possible.

The territory I fought for each day wasn't the densely populated areas with lots of stay-at-home parents, retirement communities, or even neighborhoods that had lots of mansions. It was a busy downtown area with a police station, fire station and bank. I could make more in one hour visiting those three places than I could walking the other areas for six hours.

I knew how to work those three locations. Police officers hated the idea of me walking in unfamiliar neighborhoods alone. I leveraged their concern for my safety to sell more coupons. At the fire station I could always find a handful of harmless yet hungry men who were a little bored with downtime between calls, happy to indulge a young woman in a flirty chat. And bankers—well, they fully appreciated a good bargain and always had several people more than willing to part with their money for a discounted meal and an excuse to enjoy their lunch break together.

All of this contradicted the supposed payoff offered by retirement communities whose members had little disposable income and more than enough time to cook their own meals. And the busy moms who opened the door frazzled that I'd woken up the baby they had *finally* gotten to sleep and were completely uninterested in going to a restaurant with said grumpy child. As for those big homes on the hill that clearly had plenty of money to splurge with, no one was home during daylight hours and the hills made slow going on foot. I may have been young and in shape, but I hated to waste my time even then.

By accident I had discovered personas—fictional representations of real buyers that can be used to segment prospects and fine-tune messaging. Crude, incomplete, not well researched personas, but buying attributes nonetheless.

Years later, having conducts hundreds of persona interviews and all different types of research projects for clients such as NetProspex (acquired by Dun and Bradstreet), Waters Corporation and Click Software, I've come to appreciate how instrumental early insights are to accelerating revenue traction and training sales teams.

Within the first year of graduation I had accidently learned my first two real-world lessons about marketing—effective content development and building buyer insights. First, I secured spending money by working in the writing center editing research papers and helping students meet word count minimums without torturing their poor professors. Then, I learned how to target the right buyers by going door-to-door. I was starting to be a marketer and I didn't even know it.

Pretty soon the weather started to get cold and the allure of knocking on doors was waning. I briefly held a "real job" selling employee leasing services but hated it. Expectations were low and I was bored staring at my computer screen for most of the day. Determined not to leave Massachusetts I took a job temping. This was only after asking my father to pay for graduate school and hearing him laughing so heartily, I could feel the house shake all the way across the ocean in Kenya, where he was living. Lesson number three of being a marketer—get resourceful when the funds run out!

It turned out that my first temp job was more than a stepping-stone to something else. I took a job working as an administrator at Powersoft, a hot technology company with truly inspirational leadership and exploding growth. When I started, I literally sat in the hallway because there was no other floor space. I spent my days organizing contracts, setting up meetings and trying to sound smart in a room full of far more experienced professionals. For some unexplainable reason, the head of the channel sales group took a liking to me and my administrative job grew.

It started slowly at first, invited to sit in on contract negotiations. Then I was asked to take a stab at writing the first draft of a partner communication. I quickly started asking for more responsibility by offering to run a meeting when a conflict arose for my boss, and eventually recommending program options of my own. Pretty soon, my boss gave me a list of important partners to manage and I was on the hunt to recruit new ones. It was the beginning of my career in channel sales, where I would spend years exceeding quota at software companies and helping to motivate partners to sell and support various technologies.

A few years later, with a little too much arrogance but a sincere desire to help, I complained that the channels function I was now running needed more of marketing's focus. Despite a very active marketing team, the channels team I ran was pretty much on our own. We had to write our own collateral, develop our own sales tools and push through our own pricing. I was loud enough and eager enough that they told me to go for it. I learned two things that year. First, marketing was a lot harder than I thought. And two, I *loved* it.

Because I didn't know any better, I did things my way. Maybe it's because I didn't take a single marketing class until I was many years into my career. Or maybe it was because I was trained to think like an analyst in college. Or perhaps my years having a quota—first selling restaurant coupons, then selling software through partners—made me sensitive to buying cycles. But most likely it was due to all those things that I turned out to be a successful, albeit slightly unconventional, marketer who cared more about growth than I did doing things the "right way." While I was meeting revenue and lead goals, many of my colleagues were not—and they were not alone. Similar troubles exist to this day.

Despite all our progress embracing digital technologies, advancing our mobile strategies and cementing our seat at the boardroom table, marketers still struggle.

FACT: Content output increased 35% per channel across 2015, but content engagement decreased by 17%.[2]

FACT: 74% of companies that miss lead and revenue goals don't have documented personas.[3]

FACT: Cross-functionally aligned organizations have 19% faster revenue growth and 15% higher profitability.[4] Yet only 50% of companies even have a shared definition of a lead.[5]

Although not a formally trained marketing student, I was an avid reader. On my journey I read many great books as I tried to figure out why what I did was working, and what more I could try. These books inspired me to do research, embrace my partners in sales, build advocates and dive deeply into buyer insights. But none of them told me how to do it! The advice in those books was good—but it wasn't enough.

Unleash Possible is a prescriptive guide for growth marketers of high-consideration offerings who want to forge productive relationships with sales and product development. It's a step-by-step handbook of what I've done during the last two decades to bridge the gap between buyers and revenue. In each chapter we'll cover a key concept, review a case study and map out critical how-to guidelines for applying what you've learned to your organization.

Now for the big secret: I'm sharing this with you because there isn't a single tactic in the entire book that you can't do. It's not about how much money you have, or how big or small your team has become. I promise you can't do everything on your wish list, but you can do everything that's important if you commit. This book will help you

---

2 Source: The Content Marketing Paradox Revisited, by Track Maven, 2016

3 Source: Understanding B2B Buyers 2016 Benchmark Study

4 https://www.siriusdecisions.com/Blog/2015/May/Summit-2015-Highlights-The-Economics-of-Alignment.aspx

5 http://www.marketingcharts.com/traditional/only-1-in-2-companies-say-sales-marketing-have-a-formal-definition-of-a-qualified-lead-39775/

decide what to say no to, and where and how to apply your passion. Ultimately, it will help you attract not just more buyers, but the right ones. Above all, I hope it helps you fall in love with marketing the way I did years ago, and unleash what's possible in your organization.

SECTION 1:

MOTIVATION & METRICS

CHAPTER 1

Culture: Go Beyond Candy Walls

If you want to attract marketing talent and create relentless drive in your team, stop focusing on candy walls, smoothie bars and Ping-Pong tournaments and instead put your passion into empowerment. The ability to make an impact is what really attracts and retains high performers.

My own test of this came midway through my career while I was working for a software company in the data management space. When I joined the company we were a market leader in our space and growing very quickly. I started with a team of one, me, and within months had a handful of staff members. I'd been given responsibility to lead product launches and assigned critical task force leadership roles. In short, my contributions to the company were significant and I felt recognized for my work. I was making a difference. A year into my time at this company, we were acquired by a larger database company. At first this was exciting. My team grew, and I took on responsibility for new product lines and participated as a member of the transition team. After a few months, however, everything changed. The company was getting ready for another ownership pivot and in the process day-to-day operations went into hibernation. Growth was no longer the objective; rather, we adopted a new mantra: stay steady with shrinking resources. We stopped experimenting with new programs and we laid off staff. I rolled with all of it until the day I realized my mission was to maintain the status quo.

My wake-up call came after a proposal my task force had spent months researching was presented to the executive committee. We received lavish praise for our work, but when it came down to implementing the change, we were told no. We weren't asking for any money. We weren't asking for additional resources. We had found ways to do more with less, but the company was gearing up to be sold to an even larger organization than the previous acquisition, and in this scenario, change was considered a detractor to the mission of being sold. I left the meeting devastated.

By all standards I was a high achiever. I had hit multiple growth milestones, I had won quarterly achievement awards, I was invited to participate in strategic discussions. I felt respected, but was being asked to go "on hold." Whether this was for weeks, or months, wasn't clear.

It was at just that moment that I decided to leave the company. What many people did not realize is that just four weeks earlier I had found out I was pregnant with my youngest son. Here I was at a stable job where very little was being asked of me. I was the primary financial support for my family and I was pregnant. Many people would have taken that scenario as a gift and coasted through the next few months. I simply couldn't bring myself to be satisfied with holding back. I wasn't at all sure anyone at the fast-paced companies I was attracted to would hire me pregnant, but it was a chance I had to take. I left that company the next week. As I look back, I'm still not sure whether my move was brave or crazy, but I know in my heart I had no real choice. I was a passionate growth driver and I couldn't be put on hold.

That moment taught me an important lesson about organizational culture that I carried throughout my career: Creating a culture of achievement, accountability and satisfaction is not easy, but when the right balance is struck, remarkable things happen. Culture has a big bearing on achievement. When it is missing, your best talent will leave—or worse, become mediocre. This is true across your organization, but especially in the marketing department—where we must hold our team accountable for balancing the art and science of marketing, where glory is far easier to measure in sales and where diversity is required but difficult to maintain.

SEVEN LEVERS OF EMPOWERMENT

Across my career I have worked with, and for, a very diverse set of companies. I've found the following seven levers universal across businesses large and small where growth, accountability and passion drive results.

1. Balance the art and science of marketing

In our quest for using data to make decisions, we've swung the pendulum too far. If we can't measure it, we're unwilling to experiment with it. The truth is, in marketing, emotion plays an instrumental role in connecting with our audience. We must value creativity as much as data science.

Marketing is about balancing the art and science of persuasion. Buyers make decisions with emotion and then look for rational data to support their choice.

- ○ Campaigns with purely emotional content **performed about twice as well** (31% vs. 16%) than those with only rational content; and those that were purely emotional did a little better (31% vs 26%) than those that mixed emotional and rational content.[6]

- ○ Personal value will provide **2x the impact** than business value will on a B2B purchase.[7]

If we ignore either end of that spectrum we convert fewer prospects to customers.

When I think about the most successful teams I've had the privilege to be a part of I'm struck by some important observations.

- ○ The people on the team weren't smarter than other teams.
- ○ Our budgets weren't any bigger.
- ○ The products and services we were selling weren't more differentiated.

But we displayed two critical attributes:

1. We highly valued creativity—to experiment, to learn and to be open to change.
2. We held a firm commitment to using what worked, not what we liked.

---

6 http://www.neurosciencemarketing.com/blog/articles/emotional-ads-work-best.htm

7 https://www.cebglobal.com/marketing-communications/b2b-emotion. html?referrerTitle=Surfacing%20Emotions

Yes, we measured relentlessly, but we didn't only rely on numeric measurement to hold ourselves accountable. We trusted the instincts of our experts. We relied on each other. We cared about emotion as much as conversion rates.

To make this a reality, allow your organization to try things that can't easily be measured. Give people the space and resources to think, not just analyze. Reward intelligent risk taking, rather than punish it, and don't be afraid to reward the creative as much as we reward the measured.

For example, while leading a team at a multi-billion dollar company, I realized that despite going after a new market segment, our team was playing it too safe. While many excellent ideas were generated, brainstorms were quickly dismissed as too risky. To counter the risk-averse culture, I added a "risk-taking" component to quarterly business objectives against which bonus payments were calculated for every member of my team. It sent a very clear statement. Not only is it OK to take risk, you are in fact expected to do it.

2. Respect marketing as a discipline

I'll never forget the look of shock on my boss's face the first time he was introduced by a member of the executive team as "leading the art department." Mike, my boss, was the Vice President of Marketing for a technology company with a long career and many credentials. While he, like most of my marketing colleagues, is proficient at PowerPoint AutoShapes and can draw a mean stick figure, you could hardly consider us traditional artists.

While marketing has made tremendous progress over the years in finding ways to drive and measure revenue impact, there hasn't been a single B2B company I've spoken with in the last 24 months where marketing leadership didn't lament, "Everyone thinks they can do marketing." In fact, the sentiment is surprisingly widespread.

It's evident in board meetings where everyone votes on logo design. The long list of people who need to review every press release bears witness to it. It's present in the unspoken assumption that marketing needs permission to speak with customers. It's felt every time a salesperson tells marketing what events they should attend.

As marketers we love input and we certainly don't have a monopoly on great ideas. In fact, we're pretty good about asking what you think. However, it's all too easy to cross the line between collaboration and dictating. The most effective businesses make sure marketing is empowered and feels respected for their expertise. Show your marketing team that you trust them, a lot. It matters more than you think.

3. Participatory decision making, not consensus building

As a strategic marketing consultant, one of the most important services I can offer clients is my advice. Most times, clients take that advice, but occasionally they don't. When they don't it's rarely because they disagree with the thinking behind my recommendation; it's because they can't get consensus from everyone about how to implement the concept.

Consensus building is often the death of good ideas, whether it's applied to consultant advice or to internal discussions. When we operate with the rule that in order to move forward, everyone must think the idea is good, we slow down our ability to execute. What's more, our campaigns, messages and brand get watered down to their least common denominator—wildly ineffective in a competitive environment.

There are important times when accepting a decision with which you disagree, or pushing forward without full consensus, is the right course of action.

- Will the person making this decision learn something important by making it without causing irreversible and significant damage to the business? If the answer is yes, let them make the decision.

- Is the logic behind the recommendation sound? While your gut might be mumbling that the decision is wrong, sound logic should not be ignored. None of us has a crystal ball—we must trust the data we have and the collective experience of our team.

- Do you lack conviction in your recommendation? If you are operating on incomplete information, or outside your domain expertise, think hard before pushing back on the decision maker. It's OK to test their conviction, but don't get in the way of their progress.

Healthy organizations encourage ideation, collection of feedback and debate, but they let the domain experts make the final call. I call this *participatory decision making*.

4. Build swarms around change – the 10% rule

As leaders, we need to inform what marketing is trying to achieve, not dictate how to get there. We do this by painting an inspiring vision and enabling a groundswell to bring it to life. The problem is that we often assume that the message filters from a leadership team to the balance of the organization instead of creating a formal construct that encourages the change. Research shows that in order to affect significant behavior change, we need 10% of the group to participate.

In 2007, German biologists Jens Kause and Dr. John Dyer held an experiment that brought together 200 people in a large room. The group was told to keep moving—nothing else. Left alone, the group moved in a disorganized manner. And then the leaders changed the game. Twenty of the participants were told to move toward a specific target spot in the room. Those 20 people were dispersed throughout the group and could move toward the target but not tell anyone they had been given instructions. There was nothing marking the target and no signage pointing the way. And yet, in minutes the entire 200-person group had moved toward the target. After experimenting with various participation levels, the 10% rule was born. (*Thanks to Elisa French for providing the English translation of the article relating the research.*)

Think about the implications—it only takes 10% of an organization to create a swarm.

This makes total sense when you think about what happens when you get off the airplane in an unfamiliar airport. Those walking off the plane follow the mass of people walking toward the baggage claim area. Also consider the last web seminar you attended: After the first couple of people started asking questions, did more follow?

What if you could harness the power of human swarm dynamics to accelerate fundamental improvement in your organization?

I believe you can, though it may not seem easy. The environment within which you must recreate the experiment is not static. Your peers are not locked in a room. Moving in the same direction for a few feet is much easier than over the course of several miles. And unlike the imperative of walking toward a target, transformation objectives are often complex. While all this is true, you can replicate the principal of the experiment within the context of your marketing team to achieve remarkable results.

Here's how I've seen it work.

1. **Recruit ambassadors** — In the biology experiment, the stakes were low—"walk toward the North corner." In a business environment, you can't simply say "start selling more" or "build a better product" and make it so. You need to embrace ambassadors on the journey toward creating lasting change. You don't need everyone to believe, just 10%. These are your ambassadors. Other research supports this notion. For example, Malcolm Gladwell observed similar results across many case studies in his book *The Tipping Point*.

2. **Articulate a clear direction** — In the experiment above, 10% were told clearly to walk toward a target. The swarm worked because they understood fully what direction to follow. In your business, charity or family dynamic, vision and strategy will rarely be as clear cut as "walk toward the North corner," but the more your ambassadors can understand their mission, the more likely a swarm will follow.

3. **Keep obstacles out of the way** — Ambassadors led the pack because they could. Similarly, people followed instinctively because they can. But what if a table had been set with cookies in one portion of the room? What if a pile of rocks had blocked a passage? Would the swarm have formed as neatly? Not only must we create a clear direction, we must empower ambassadors to take obstacles out of the way (and help remove them ourselves) to clear the path for their followers.

4. **Reinforce the swarm** — If instead of walking to the corner of a room, you wanted the participants to walk 10 miles—would the experiment have the same effect? In business, to transform an organization you need to sustain progress over time. That means, to keep the swarm progressing, you must reinforce behavior by providing compelling new incentives to keep moving forward. Don't forget to replace ambassadors who are tired and give out after the third mile, or the eighth. In effect, you have to keep creating little swarms that move you toward your designated goal. Swarms are relatively easy to get started, but maintaining them takes patience and focused effort.

5. **Embrace diversity**

   My 10-year-old, Johnny, reached over the breakfast table one morning and asked, "Mom, what do you see in this toaster strudel?" Each of our children has a unique personality and approach to the world around him. Johnny is my "creative boy." That means he tells the best stories (aka lies), but he also has a vivid imagination that makes you giggle as you are transported to another place alongside him. (In case you are wondering, Johnny saw a whale spouting water and a frog in his toaster strudel that morning.)

Just like our children, each adult has a unique approach to the world. Our employees problem-solve in different ways because of their unique perspective. Where he saw animals, I saw a person leaning over in a field with the sun rising behind them. This is a good thing.

What do you see?

In business, when you want to innovate, you must foster different approaches. In marketing, innovation is mandatory, as we often can't afford to spend our way toward standing out of the crowd.

We need to recruit people who have a wide array of experiences and perspectives to collaborate and share their visions. We want our team to look at the toaster strudel and see different possibilities—but the magic of collaboration isn't that we see different things, it's rather that we help each other see our diverse visions. I can now clearly see the whale and he can see the farmer.

The ability not only to think of new visions, but to share those visions across the team makes for powerful creativity that, if harnessed, propels your new campaign, designs exciting new products and even makes current processes more efficient.

Of course, sometimes different personalities clash and create conflict. Leaders often eliminate talented people who operate differently to avoid this conflict. At stages in my career I have been guilty of getting rid of individuals thinking I was doing the right thing for the team as a whole. But this doesn't pass the Toaster Strudel Test. I wouldn't trade any of my boys who all saw different possibilities in their morning treat—the creative one, my natural-born salesman, the soft-spoken hard worker or the analyst. Why wouldn't I value the diversity in my employees as much as I appreciate it in my children?

Don't misunderstand me—culture does matter. A perpetually negative or difficult person can be toxic. Don't live with poison because you are afraid of making a mistake. My point is rather that in the name of culture, we often judge too quickly. Before letting someone go, voluntarily or by mandate, think about what they are contributing. Does their way of thinking force us to be better? If the answer is yes, even some of the time, take pause and evaluate your next steps carefully. This is equally true when we recruit new members to a team. Do you want a clone of your existing talent? Or do you want someone who might push a different point of view?

The next time you tackle a new opportunity think about team dynamics. Can your team pass the Toaster Strudel Test? Or will they all see the same picture?

6. **Stop collecting NOs; encourage yes-ortunities**

As sales and marketing professionals, our job is to get a YES.

○ YES, I'll buy a ticket to your conference.

○ YES, I'll purchase your product.

○ YES, I'll renew my services contract for another year.

In our quest for the big YES we get a lot of NOs. Many professionals accept NO as part of the price we pay for being in sales and marketing. Most people don't open our emails. Most meetings don't lead to a second get-together. Most phone calls end without agreement about how to move forward. We even go as far as to consider collecting NOs as evidence that we are working hard. Sadly, that is the completely wrong way to look at it. The reason we get so many NOs is that we focus too much on the end decision and not on all the little opportunities to get a YES along the way. Unfortunately, despite a great deal of discussion about mapping the buyer's journey, as a whole, our profession has made limited progress.

Just a couple of days ago someone tweeted a link to an article that got my attention. I excitedly clicked the link. Before I could more than blink, a pop-up window appeared demanding I sign up for their email newsletter. I hadn't even read one line of the article, on a site I'd never visited before, and they wanted me to sign up? Boy, they were asking for a NO. Still interested in the article I tried to close the subscription box and read the article anyway, only to find that I couldn't read the article unless I subscribed. So I gave a fake email address and read the piece.

It felt like a YES to the person reporting subscription rates, but it was a very clear NO. They should have let me read the article and followed up with another piece of relevant content. Maybe I would have said YES to reading more from them. But I wasn't ready to say YES to being on their email distribution list. I'm guessing email subscription rates was their intended metric, when return-visitor rates might have been more effective.

Lest you think I'm picking on marketers, consider a sales scenario that happened the same day. I was observing a prospecting call at a client's office. The introductions had gone well and the salesperson had piqued the audience's interest at least enough to stay on the phone. They even got the prospect to identify their current solution and a pain point or two. Instead of inviting this prospect to a web seminar being hosted the next day that would directly address their pain, the salesperson started talking about pricing and competitive differentiators of their offering. The prospect ended the call and no natural next step was engaged. They missed their yes-ortunity.

The two scenarios above are obvious examples of what you don't want to do. In fact, it's likely you would roll your eyes at either of them. But I'm willing to bet that if you took a critical eye toward reviewing all your activity, you would find more subtle ways you are inviting NOs.

Here's the good news! This is an easy issue to address. Early in my career I decided to stop expecting NO and to start planning every encounter to get a YES.

A YES might start off as simple as accepting a LinkedIn connection request. Or it could be as complex as agreeing to a 30-minute follow-up phone call. Helping employees on their journey is a careful game of small moves, just as it is with buyers. All you have to do is reorient yourself to focus on the next step, not the end goal—sharing an idea, connecting on social, a second meeting, a proposal, problem identification, securing budget, etc.

We need to train our team to ask themselves, in every encounter, what they could offer that this person is almost certain to say yes to. We must incentivize them to know that this is the move they should make.

The road to closing business is paved with lots of small yes-ortunities. Help your team stay aware of them, and navigate the journey.

7. **Believe you know enough**

In a world where data is literally everywhere, analysis paralysis is a very real disease. In an earnest quest to learn before we act, we naturally seek out various viewpoints. Where some fall victim to inaction is when they fail to recognize when to stop collecting data. There comes a time when you know enough, when learning more will not make a better decision, and when a delay will in fact create a default decision instead of an active one. In these instances, get comfortable with imperfect information and trust that you know enough.

CASE STUDY: NOT READY, NOT SET, GO!

I had just started a new job as VP, Marketing, at a technology startup that had no customers. On my first, day the CEO informed me we would be launching the product during an industry event in May less than five months away. It was the perfect venue for our audience and if we missed this May deadline there wasn't another opportunity like it for an additional six months.

We had no logo, no website, no collateral, no customer-facing messaging, and no marketing staff. We had less than very little time to create a brand, build evangelists, launch a website from scratch, test messaging and hire a team. I said yes.

We had no time to crawl. We had to run fast, and almost everything had to be done in parallel. The first thing I did was assemble a team. I hired three full-time resources with very different skill sets: a writer and messaging expert as our product marketer, a marketing automation and demand-nurturing workhorse, and a project manager with event skills. A couple of months later we would also hire a product manager to interface with the engineering team.

In addition, I tapped into external expertise. We hired a design agency to develop a brand standard, logo and corporate website framework. I also hired a PR agency to help us engage with evangelists. I broke with traditional protocol and built into the contract having our primary account manager at the agency join us on-site for one day each week. I wanted them to feel a part of my team, not an extension of it.

Although a couple of team members had worked together before, most didn't know one another. We had to build rapport while running full steam ahead—not only with one another but with the rest of the organization.

With so much at stake, the company was understandably focused on and demanding of my marketing team. What we were building would be the foundation for who we were in the eyes of the market. We were a new entrant to an established market, with very few proof points. Marketing had to immediately build trust across the organization and among ourselves. We became obsessively transparent and relentlessly decisive.

We designed our workspace to be collaborative but also to respect personal space. I had originally wanted a completely open layout, but the team pushed back. They loved working with others but knew they needed heads-down time to meet our aggressive schedules. We accommodated both by placing half-height walls between desks and two open areas for brainstorming. We had lunch together 2–3 days a week to get to know one another, and we spent at least half of every meeting in open discussions and addressing at-risk items.

We held a weekly ideation and status meeting so our external partners in PR and the design agency could join us, but daily ad hoc progress discussions happened without much effort. Our very talented product marketing resource and I developed messaging and, due to our compressed timeframe and virtually no database, we hired a research company to host focus groups. We needed to be decisive about our core value proposition, differentiation and go-to-market messaging, and the only way to move fast was to talk to a lot of buyers, fast.

In parallel, our demand generation and project manager began building our marketing operations infrastructure, securing data, selecting a database and purchasing the space we needed for our launch event.

We took the output from the messaging focus group discussions and presented it to the executive team and the board. I went into the meeting prepared to go to battle, expecting loud disagreements about our core messages. To my shock, it didn't happen—the team trusted us because we'd followed a rigorous testing process and competitive analysis. The team's input was minor and was provided swiftly.

With this backdrop, we quickly moved to creating the visual components of our brand. Here I miscalculated—I had been prepared to go to battle on the messaging, but had wildly underestimated how strongly the team would feel about our brand colors and logo. Unlike messaging, I had worked with a professional agency on the design, but we hadn't established focus groups. As a result, we had meeting after meeting debating our colors and logo.

The marketing team's progress was at a standstill. Unless we could get signoff, we couldn't build collateral templates, start designing the website or even produce business cards and the company letterhead. What made things worse was the fact that everyone was arguing based on their personal preferences, and emotions were running high.

May was looming and I realized I had to do something. Holding one last input session, I narrowed down two palette options and two logo options. Instead of seeking consensus, I begged for trust. Based only on my two choices, we stopped iterating and the CEO and CTO cofounders made a selection.

It would prove to this day to be the most challenging component of any product launch I've ever had to manage, but from that point forward we got back to running toward our launch goal, and we never stopped.

We built the website. We built trusted influencer relationships. We briefed the analysts. We created presentations, data sheets, demos, call scripts, and beta customer case studies. You name it, we did it in record time.

In the end, all the goals we had established for launch were met or exceeded:

- We were included in 53% of all media articles in our category, appearing as an established vendor with a unique value proposition.
- We secured a placement as a Gartner Cool Vendor and enjoyed several analyst and influencer endorsements.

○ We qualified and nurtured 75 sales opportunities.

○ We established a sustainable thought leadership positioning platform that others started to adopt.

Those first five months were the beginning, but they built a foundation and bonds that still exist today.

HOW-TO GUIDELINES: SEVEN COMPONENTS OF A PRODUCTIVE BRAINSTORM SESSION

An essential component of a collaborative work culture is the often-dreaded brainstorming session. Holding a brainstorm is easy. Holding a productive brainstorm session, however, takes effort. After lots of experimentation, I've found that the following tips can ensure brainstorm sessions that result in good ideas:

1. **Right-size the group.**

   Brainstorm sessions need a variety of ideas to be effective, but with too large a group it's difficult to make progress, and with too small a group ideas stagnate. I've found teams of 4–8 are ideal. If you want to solicit feedback from more participants, I recommend breaking the larger group into smaller teams that can report back to the others for final ideation and prioritization.

2. **Remember that quantity does matter in a brainstorm session.**

   Although you may only select a small numbers of ideas to execute, it helps to have lots of ideas to consider, since sometimes the best concepts come from combining components of multiple incomplete notions. In the early stages, don't worry about eliminating untenable ideas or duplications—the more, the better.

3. **Give context in advance.**

   Don't wait for the session to start to let people know what they will be discussing. The best ideas build off each other and coming into the session with some preliminary thoughts will use your time wisely. Make sure you schedule 60–90 minutes to provide enough time to build ideas on one another.

4. Provide guardrails.

Be clear with participants about what you are trying to solve for. It can be small, such as an upcoming event theme, or large, such as attacking a new market. In either case, make sure the team knows of the parameters in advance. While you don't want to exclude ideas with highly limited constraints, you want people to feel like their ideas have a chance of being executed.

5. Use a facilitator to document ideas.

A facilitator does not need to have all the ideas, but they need to be good at soliciting participation from everyone in the room while remaining focused on the goals at hand. Ideally, assign someone to guide the conversation who has some domain expertise but will not dominate the conversation. The guide should use a variety of techniques to solicit ideas such as individual list building, group whiteboarding, and voting. The specific techniques aren't as important as ensuring that there are a variety of ways to capture ideas.

I like to start each session by reminding everyone why we are in the room and what role each of them plays in our success. If the opportunity we are addressing is not complex, then I go straight to capturing ideas on a whiteboard. For more complex ideation I give people a notepad and some time to jot down their own thoughts before sharing them with the larger group.

Once you feel you've maxed out useful ideation (usually 20–30 minutes), take a break. Encourage people to leave the room, grab a cold drink, and shake off the discussion. Even just 5 minutes of break is an important step. Once everyone returns to the room, open the floor for a few minutes once again for additional ideation.

Next, cross off ideas that are duplicates and begin to scope the effort required for each. Don't worry about being precise in your scope—this should simply be a crude effort to help assess the viability of each idea.

I like to use two factors, budget and difficulty level, as measures to indicate a small, medium, or large effort.

Budget Key:

$ – low or no budget required

$$ – moderate budget required

$$$ – significant expense

Difficulty Key:

Small – existing resources have time to allocate to this effort

Medium – executing on this idea will require deprioritizing other efforts

Large – new resources (internal or external) will be required

For example, if we were looking to capture mindshare at an industry trade show, our brainstorm might look something like this:

Idea	Budget	Difficulty
Start a flash mob during the exhibit floor opening reception	$	L
#RideInStyle Hire limo service to drive key influencers and speakers from the airport to the conference venue	$$	S
Put Buzzword bingo cards in attendee bags and give prizes away in booth	$$$	M

Once the crude scoping is complete, you can move on to prioritization.

6. **Prioritize as a second step.**

Don't eliminate ideas while you are ideating. Instead get all the ideas documented and prioritize them during the second half of the meeting. I find prioritization most effective using a voting technique. Give all participants three stickers (not red—you'll see why later) and ask them to write their initials on them. Then ask the group to get up and put their stickers next to the ideas they feel will be most impactful and should be executed. Let them know they can use all three of their votes for a single idea or spread them across three different concepts. Now give everyone one red sticker. This is their veto vote. They should put it on ideas they feel are dangerous, completely off goal or impossible to pull off. Most people will not use their veto vote, but those who feel strongly have a couple of minutes to put it next to a highly rated idea.

Once everyone has used their stickers, focus your conversation on the ideas that got the most votes. If any received a veto vote, allow that person to explain why they want to veto the idea.

Don't fully dismiss those ideas that only got a small amount of support. Once you've discussed those that had high support, give everyone in the room the opportunity to voice a defense for ideas that didn't make the cut.

7. **Assign follow-up tasks.**

The biggest criticism I hear about brainstorming sessions is that ideas never get implemented. Don't let that happen—assign specific follow-up tasks with due dates and a responsible party. Next steps might include more fully scoping out the effort, securing budget or jumping into execution mode.

Building a culture of empowerment is feasible, no matter the size or maturity of your organization. I hope these tips have given you the courage to start implementing the tenets of growth, accountability, and passion to drive real business results.

CHAPTER 2

Nontraditional Metrics Marketing Must Own

I'm the type of person who measures everything. I know how many proposals I convert to revenue. I know the profile of the executives who hire me compared to those who take free advice. I know how many hours each type of engagement takes to complete. I even know how many chocolate truffles it takes to get through a difficult conference call.

Thanks is owed to my dad, the primary reason for my number obsession. You should have seen the charts he had drawn counting down to retirement; they were a work of art.

This is a shared obsession among my community of marketers. We become fixated with open and click-through rates. We fret over keyword ranking. We're thrilled when our email subscription rates skyrocket, and for good reason. These are metrics related to the tools of our trade which we must learn to master. However, these are not the measurements marketing should be held accountable against. When we concentrate exclusively on them, we lose focus on our core mission: to drive business growth.

In this chapter we'll explore the critical business metrics for which marketing must have ownership to build credibility and drive the organization forward. These business metrics tell a bigger story than the transactional metrics that are typically measured. We focus on business metrics because they provide insight that can specifically be acted on and have a direct impact on growth.

SALES METRICS

I'm always shocked when I speak to sales and marketing professionals and find that they have very few shared metrics, aside from revenue or profitability. In many organizations, marketers are responsible for leads, unique website visitors and brand awareness. The sales team is responsible for the length of the sales cycle, win rate and closing bottom-line revenue. On the surface this makes perfect sense—divide and conquer. But in fact, it's this harsh division of labor that leads to unhealthy tension and inefficiencies.

Leads-to-First-Meeting/Demo

While I never met a sales team that didn't want more leads, what they really want is more opportunities. Executive pressure to increase leads often comes at a cost; the passing of poor-quality leads that don't align to target markets and buying intent.

Marketers must be responsible for the ratio of leads-to-first-meeting (sometimes labeled as sales-qualified leads, or SQL). When we hold ourselves accountable to maintain or improve this ratio, we start to focus on the marketing activities that matter toward this goal. For example, we start training salespeople in how to follow up on specific types of leads. We make sure the sales team is well armed with proper incentives for their first meeting, such as assessments, research reports, use cases and persona-based presentations and demo scripts. We ensure that what they present during those initial meetings leaves a lasting impression. We relentlessly follow up with sales to make sure they are quickly picking up the lead handoff we sent them. As a result of focusing on the right metric, we in turn focus on the right activities needed to find and deliver better-quality leads in the first place.

To do this well means we have to balance our budgets without obsessing over our cost-per-lead (CPL). When we make decisions based on CPL, we head down a dangerous path. I might be able to significantly reduce my cost-per-lead, but at what cost? Are 100 leads costing $5 that produce 6 opportunities really better than 100 leads costing $20 that produce 28 opportunities? What we should be measuring is cost-per-conversion-to-opportunity.

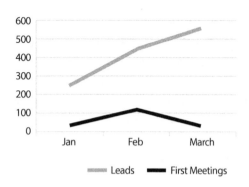

Looking at the example raises some obvious questions. What happened in March? Did sales get distracted? Did we introduce a new lead source that tanked?

If we're only measured on lead volume, we don't ask ourselves these very important questions. We need to understand what is resulting in a qualified opportunity, and what is driving meaningless quantity. Don't forget—it takes bandwidth and resources from sales and your lead nurturing efforts to work new leads. As a marketer, would you rather spend resources working 1,000 leads that convert to 10 meetings or efficiently delivering 100 leads that convert to 10 meetings?

Of course there is a minimum threshold of activity we all must maintain, and that is different for each business. But marketing's credibility with sales and the overall organizational efficiency is best when the ratio is lower.

Length of Time in Each Stage of the Buying Process

The second metric I recommend implementing is the length of time for each stage in the buying process (typically measured in days). Even those enlightened marketers who measure the conversion from lead-to-first-meeting or SQL rarely measure anything between the first meeting and the percentage of overall leads that result in revenue. This is a huge missed opportunity. The work we do to lay out the buyer's journey should be coupled with a measurement of the effectiveness of marketing's impact on leads at each stage. Seek to evaluate whether we're reducing the amount of time each buyer spends in each stage. Doing so can motivate us to improve the buyer's experience with helpful content and resources that match their needs. It gives us a chance to improve the delivery and format of this content. Ultimately, it allows us to better train the sales team to use the tools we've worked so hard to build.

In the next example there are 5 stages to the buyer's journey that are tracked in the CRM system. You can see average number of days between cycles trending over time. For example, you can see in the chart that the average number of days in proposal stage is dropping steadily over time. That would indicate one of two things. First, we are getting better at qualifying opportunities and sending proposals when they are most likely to be addressed by the prospect. Second, we may be providing tools that help our buyer champion sell internally more effectively, i.e., ROI calculators, business case builders, etc. By tracking this metric the team is held accountable to track and improve against both of those levers.

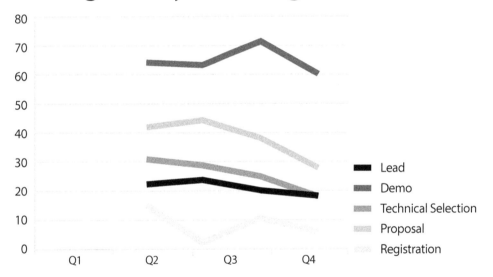

Average # Days Per Stage

It can take a long time to see an impact on buyer stage duration, so don't seek to measure this factor too frequently. Expect 2–3 full sales cycles before you see significant difference. That means, if your average sales process is 30 days, you'll need 60–90 days to see the full impact of any new programs you implement.

Win rate

My final recommended sales-oriented metric is very important: win rate. Too many marketers are afraid to take ownership of the company's average win rate. It's deemed outside of marketing's control and often viewed as a direct result of the sales team's skills. While sales effectiveness certainly plays a part, sharing ownership of our win rate can significantly change the behavior of marketers in a way that focuses us on results.

When we seek to impact win rates, we build content for the last stretch of the sales process. We invest in training programs that better align sales actions to target personas. We even pay closer attention to our competition and work to build a differentiated offering. Best of all, the organization gives us the emotional permission and resources to do it when we are committing to improving this critical metric.

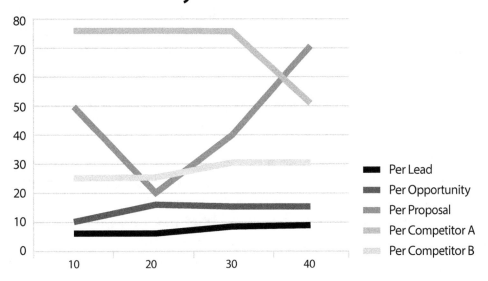

Let's take a look at an example above, which compares the average win rate on the vertical axis over time on the horizontal axis. Examining aggregate win rate is helpful—but it's most effective when we watch it over time and take a more granular look at:

- ○ Win rate per lead source
- ○ Win rate per opportunity
- ○ Win rate per proposal
- ○ Win rate per competitor

With these details, we can start to see patterns emerge about where we are losing and where we are winning. This allows us to replicate success and learn from loss.

For example, check out the sharp decline in win rate against Competitor A from Q3 to Q4. We would ask ourselves, What's going on there? Perhaps they just released a new product, or changed their pricing. Giving ourselves an opportunity to answer this question provides clear direction on where we should apply resources in the future that will have a true impact the business.

Adoption Metrics

A marketer's job is not done once a customer places an order. We will discuss this in detail in Chapter 11, but suffice it to note for now that in order to resource appropriately it's important that we measure adoption of our offerings, not just the number of orders that have been placed.

While each product or service is unique, some measure of these three adoption metrics is critical to building loyalty and the opportunity to upsell.

1. *Time-to-Initiation.* The sooner a customer starts to gain value, the more likely they are to be satisfied. How long does it take after an order is placed for the customer to use your product or service? Be careful when you measure this not to focus on the delivery schedule, but rather the time when customers actually begin to engage. For example, you may send out login instructions within an hour of an order being placed, but if the customer doesn't log in for 30 days, your time-to-initiation is 30 days, not one hour.

2. *Percentage of Offering Used.* Some products are single function. For example, the headphones I use to record web seminars have one clear, designated use. However, many businesses offer complex products or services that have many components. When measuring this metric we are not referring to upselling additional products or services. We simply want to measure whether our customers are taking advantage of everything they have purchased. The greater their use of what's available, the more likely they will see value in the offer when it comes time to renew the contract or advocate to a peer. If only a single feature or capability is used, it's often hard to justify a repeat spend at the same budget threshold, even if that single function is valuable.

For example, I had a subscription to a suite of design tools. The product I purchased came with a rich set of capabilities, from editing photographs to illustrations. When I placed the order, I felt I was getting a very good value. But after the first year of my subscription, I had only used one of the six tools available to me. When it came time for renewal, I declined the contract renewal. There was nothing wrong with the one feature I was using, but mentally I could not continue to pay for the majority of tools and features I had never even opened.

As marketers, our goal must be to analyze when this happens, and work with our post-sales and customer service team members to ensure that our customers receive the full value for what they have purchased.

3. **Frequency of Use.** There are few products or services that a business purchases that are designed to only be used once. However, there are many instances when a specific event triggers a purchase. After that compelling reason for using the solution has passed, it's common for usage to drop considerably.

Consider this example. One client of mine was preparing for a big presentation to their board about content marketing. It was important to them to look polished and professional, so they purchased an editorial calendar tool. From the perspective of the editorial product company, things looked great. They had a motivated buyer who used the product right away for a very important meeting. The client was happy, but things soon fell apart. Their initial motivation never turned into a sustained practice of using the editorial calendar on a regular basis. Instead, they were cramming in data for quarterly updates to management. In the end, it was very hard to justify renewing the product license because there wasn't frequent use.

As marketers it's our job to make sure we have ways to measure product usage and respond to trends that we are seeing to improve retention rates and renewal rates.

While marketing is not the only function to impact adoption metrics, marketing can and should play an active part in improving them with:

- product design and in-product prompts
- enhanced expectation setting
- improved communications strategies that prompt action
- rewards and incentives for desired behavior
- qualitative research to better understand customers

Advocacy Metrics

Many organizations measure customer satisfaction. This is a useful metric and the organization as a whole should care about it. However, from a marketing perspective it does not go far enough. Most satisfied customers will never actively advocate on behalf of the organization.

Marketers should tap into and expand the group of customers who will act as advocates on their behalf. Activities advocates may engage in might include:

- Writing a review
- Making a recommendation to a friend/peer
- Sharing content
- Commenting on published content
- Speaking with journalists

Marketers should go beyond general customer satisfaction scores and be held accountable for transforming happy customers into advocates. In Chapter 15 we discuss how to set up referral programs.

Metrics should include:

Percentage of customer base who are active advocates — The raw number of customer advocates is going to change over time. Aim for a minimum of 10% of customers to be labeled as active advocates. The most successful organizations significantly overachieve that minimum threshold.

Advocate engagement — How engaged are your advocates? One way of measuring this is to set specific goals for advocacy (such as sharing content, making referrals, writing reviews or speaking with journalists). Over time, track the engagement of your advocates against these specific program goals—for example, the number of direct referrals or online reviews attained through the program.

Advocate impact — Advocacy comes with a few clear benefits that can prove the value of the program and help you to defend keeping it in place. Track metrics stemming from specific program goals, for example the number of opportunities from direct referrals, or site traffic stemming from online reviews.

Number of detractors — Not only is it important to support advocates, but it is equally important that we track and understand our detractors. Detractors are more than dissatisfied customers. They are public voices with an active mission to spread bad news about your company. Detractors may be customers, but they are just as likely to come from former customers, partners and employees. They may even be unattached influencers who simply dislike your approach to market.

When we focus our marketing measurement on business goals, rather than only on vanity metrics or transactional details, we can make better decisions related to resource allocation, priorities, budget, and ultimately tell a better story about the impact of our efforts.

SECTION 2:

SALES & MARKETING
COLLABORATION

CHAPTER 3

The Ice Cream Sundae Workshop

It's 6:00 p.m. on the last day of the quarter. My husband, David, calls, wondering when I'm coming home. I'm a little shocked to get his call—usually at this time my husband is still sleeping, getting the last couple of hours in before working the overnight shift at the *Boston Herald*. This was back in the day before children stopped us from ever sleeping and newspapers were a competitive business.

I hadn't told him I was going to be late because I figured he wouldn't even notice. It turns out he had something else in mind: he tried to surprise me by taking the night off work and having dinner waiting. Oops! We had only been married a few months and this was the first time I was going to disappoint my husband—big time. Even so, I couldn't come home for a few more hours.

At the time I was leading channel marketing for a document management software company that was growing quickly. We had a big quota to meet, and as was our tradition, sales and marketing stayed in the office together until the last order was booked during west coast business hours. We ordered pizza, broke out some cold beer and told stories, cheering for one another with every incoming order.

I'm pretty sure my husband has no memory of this incident, but I remember it vividly because it was one of the first times in my career I chose work over personal time willingly.

When I got home my husband asked what I had done that night at work. I sheepishly told him the truth. I ate pizza, had a beer and provided moral support. The orders I was personally responsible to drive had all come in by noon. He was a little confused about why I stayed, but I had no doubt about it. I was part of a team and I enjoyed staying to cheer on my "squad." It was a tradition I was happy to keep because we all felt part of the same mission.

The feeling I had that night surrounded by my colleagues is something I aimed to capture in every subsequent job. Unfortunately, it often proved difficult to find and I found myself facing resistance.

Have you ever heard marketing talk about salespeople like this?

- "Salespeople are coin-operated."
- "They are selfish, only focused on their commission and don't care that we have to struggle to meet the promises they made."
- "The laziest people in the company are salespeople who can't be bothered to look for an answer on their own."
- "Sales representatives have huge egos."

What have you heard salespeople saying things like this about marketers?

- "Marketers are clueless about what really happens in the field."
- "They keep producing content no one is ever going to use."
- "The brand police are at it again, slowing me down."

I'd love to tell you I've never spoken or overhead any of those stereotypes, but I'd be lying. The truth is, sales and marketing professionals have different DNA. Our teams are made up of many diverse people with different strengths and challenges. We're drawn to our careers for good reason, but the differences often lead to misunderstandings and snap judgments. Yet we have a single, shared mission to serve our customers. In this chapter we'll come face to face with reality about where collaboration falls apart, but more important, we'll explore an easy first step toward breaking down the barriers. (And I promise, we will get to the part about ice cream soon!)

Misalignment Is Pervasive

Research shows that cross-functionally aligned organizations have 19% faster revenue growth and 15% higher profitability.[8] Yet many sales and marketing teams suffer a subtle, yet counterproductive, tug of wills when it comes to planning, executing programs and reporting on lead conversion. While there are many reasons these teams fall out of alignment, the net result is slower growth and unnecessary tension.

In 2016 I set out to study the state of sales and marketing collaboration. I wanted to verify whether misalignment was an exaggerated myth, or a reality. From a study of over 123 organizations, the data is very clear. The chasm between sales and marketing is significant.

It would appear marketers are harder on themselves than their sales counterparts. When we asked participants to rate marketing's value to sales in the past 12 months, 49% of sales respondents said it had improved significantly, but only 20% of marketers said the same.

QUESTION: At my current employer my marketing coworkers do a superb job of supporting sales efforts. How much do you agree with this statement?

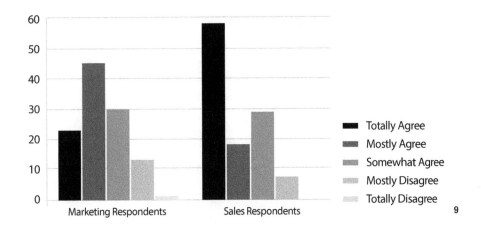

8 SiriusDecicions, https://www.siriusdecisions.com/Blog/2015/May/Summit-2015-Highlights-The-Economics-of-Alignment.aspx

9 http://marketingadvisorynetwork.com/wp-content/uploads/2016/03/Sales-and-Marketing-Collaboration-Study-June-2016.pdf

What's more, only 21% of marketing respondents agreed they do a superb job of supporting sales efforts, while 51% of sales respondents totally agreed with the statement.

QUESTION: My sales team is rewarded for supporting marketing's objectives (True or False)

% Responded True

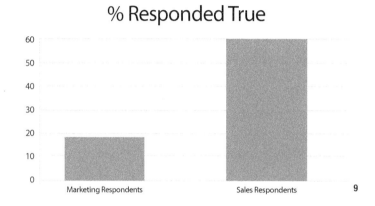

Almost 60% of sales respondents feel they are rewarded for supporting marketing objectives, while only 18% of marketers agreed.

QUESTION: Our sales reps follow up on what % of marketing-supplied leads?

95%+ Followed Up

Perhaps the most shocking misalignment is around lead follow-up, the area where sales and marketing interact most frequently. Less than 20% of marketing respondents indicated that sales follows up on 95%+ of leads delivered by marketing. Yet, sales thinks they are doing a much better job. Fifty percent of salespeople said 95%+ of sales leads delivered are followed up.

Even when it comes to sales tools, we're not aligned. The study is clear that a lot of sales tools that marketing generates are not being used by sales, but what's more surprising is how much more sales believe they use than marketing. Over 50% of salespeople responded that they use "virtually 100%" of the tools created by marketing. By striking contrast, only 15% of marketers saw it that way.

Question:

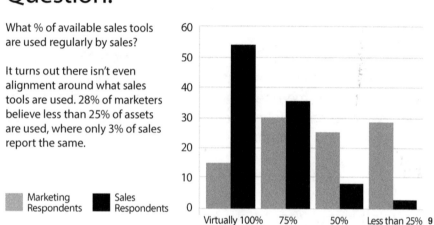

What % of available sales tools are used regularly by sales?

It turns out there isn't even alignment around what sales tools are used. 28% of marketers believe less than 25% of assets are used, where only 3% of sales report the same.

Marketing Respondents   Sales Respondents

Virtually 100%   75%   50%   Less than 25%   **9**

CASE STUDY: THE ICE CREAM SUNDAE WORKSHOP

Making changes to the sales and marketing process is difficult to achieve when the sales team isn't completely bought into the effort. Passive resistance is exactly what I found at my client, a midsized technology company.

The problem:

The sales management team had recruited me to come in on a consulting basis to objectively review and improve collaboration between their team and marketing. I had their open and full support. Yet, four weeks into the project I was facing only pockets of acceptance.

- ○ The demand generation manager felt that sales didn't follow up on all new leads despite tightening up lead qualification criteria. It was very clear the sales team was not reading much of what was being shared with them because they were regularly asking for content that already existed.

- ○ It was normal for a salesperson to pull out their phone and respond to email in weekly huddle meetings.

I had overestimated how much sales management support would drive acceptance of new processes. It was time to help the team understand *why* we were making changes, and *how* they could help accelerate the benefits of change.

The Solution:

We set up a two-hour workshop with some strict guidelines. No phones, no computers (I would provide notes) and mandatory attendance for the duration of the workshop. If something prevented a team member from being there, a teammate was assigned to conduct a 1:1 afterward to share what they learned. For the workshop to be effective I needed everyone's undivided attention.

Workshop Agenda

10 Things You Didn't Know About Your Facilitator

Though it may seem counterintuitive, I started the workshop by helping the team get to know me. I had to prove I was credible, and I had to do it in a way that was going to capture their attention. This was a mix of playful facts and achievements. When this session was replicated in other locations by employees who were well known, they altered their presentation slightly to focus on "10 Things You Didn't Know We Accomplished Together."

Get to the vanilla

If everything had been working perfectly, the workshop would not have been needed. I prevented inevitable skepticism and took eye rolling off the table by pointing out where marketing was struggling. To get this insight, I had interviewed two workshop participants in advance to ensure sincere feedback. I also made some of my own observations that the sales team might have missed, as I could see "behind-the-curtain" marketing activities they probably didn't even know were happening.

Then, to foster trust, I did the scariest thing a workshop facilitator can do: I opened the floor up to complaints. I went over to the whiteboard and asked the team to add to my list. I did so with only two constraints: First, mention a point only once, because there is no reason to repeat an issue after it was captured. Second, be specific. Don't say "leads suck." Explain the characteristics behind why leads reach the "suck" stage

I then asked them to help me build a list of things we were doing well.

Once we completed this step, I explained that we had just made the base of an ice cream sundae. It was vanilla. A little boring, but a necessary base nonetheless. I told them that together we were going to dress it up. (After all, who likes a sundae with only vanilla ice cream?)

I then showed the team the future changes we were committed to making, being careful to explain the impact each would have on the team. For each new item I provided a different ice cream flavor—five in all. For example, my scoop of strawberry was a new event strategy, and chocolate was a new lead scoring model.

Top it off

We weren't done yet. Marketing had a lot of ideas—a new email nurture campaign, an ROI assessment tool and a benchmark research study—but so too did the sales team, and I wanted them to feel accountable for sales and marketing success, not just their quota. For the balance of the workshop I put them to work. Marketing had taken a step to show we were working for sales; now it was sales' turn to show they also were willing to be working for marketing.

I explained I had purchased about a dozen different toppings choices, and for each idea they generated, they could earn a topping. Any sundae toppings that were not selected would be donated to my four boys. (I begged the group not to have any left over! Four boys hopped up on sugar is not my ideal way to end the day).

In the end I asked them to help prioritize three ideas we would execute against. It didn't matter whether these were ideas previously conceived, or were full of holes. The point of the exercise was to get the sales team thinking of marketing as part of their mission too.

In closing, while the team was enjoying their well-earned ice cream treats I went around the room and asked everyone to share one thing they would be doing differently after the day's session.

The Results

Everyone left feeling energized and feeling that we were in fact working as one team. Later that week, two other office locations asked if we could host "an ice cream sundae workshop" for their teams.

I won't pretend the workshop was a magic switch and that old habits never returned, but I can tell you with certainty it was the beginning of lasting change.

- Sales representatives started sharing more information with marketing about specific accounts. Every month marketing and sales would do an account review and brainstorm account-specific programs they could do together.
- When marketing asked to interview a customer, sales was more willing to make the introduction.
- Leads that were rejected came with a reason in the CRM system.
- Marketing and sales actively praised their coworkers when they had worked together, giving credit for closed deals not just to the salesperson, but also to the content, marketer or event that contributed.

Why did it work?

Do you have to use ice cream to get the same results? Probably not, but you should consider a program with the following characteristics:

- **Tangible** — The ice cream sundae was tangible. Everyone in the room was working for something they could touch, see, and in this case, taste. Don't underestimate the power of sensation to cement ideas into memory.

- ○ **Immediate gratification** — We held the workshop to drive lasting, long-term change, but it's hard to motivate short-term behavior in the hope that something will be better down the road. The ice cream sundae gave us something immediate to sink our teeth into (pun intended) and a reason to pay attention in the moment.

- ○ **Broad appeal** — Ice cream is appealing to just about everyone. For the more health-conscious among the group, you can have yogurt and fruit on hand to complement the more traditional topping selections.

- ○ **Participatory** — I could easily have talked for two hours about the programs we were going to run, but if I did, the audience would not feel part of the process. I gave the sales team power to influence what we built together—a necessary component to fostering change and strengthening any team.

- ○ **Memorable** — The ice cream was more than a reward for participating in the workshop—it was an analogy for the complexities of executing marketing programs that drive revenue. It cemented the concept that our prospects do not all like one flavor, and we need communication approaches as diverse as we are in our tastes. In the end, it is a reminder that sales and marketing without each other is a little bland, and that together it can be a whole lot more fulfilling.

Considering these characteristics will make sure that your workshop isn't just another meeting, and instead is a memorable, impactful session.

How To Sustain Collaboration

In Chapter 2, Nontraditional Metrics Marketing Must Own, we identified shared metrics that are an essential foundation for sustaining collaboration between marketing and sales. When seeking to facilitate the cooperation of the two groups, keep these important principles in mind.

It's not the frequency, but the variety of communications that counts.

You might be surprised to learn that more frequent meetings between sales and marketing does not always equate to better communication when it comes to reviewing campaigns.

QUESTION: How often do sales and marketing meet to review campaigns?

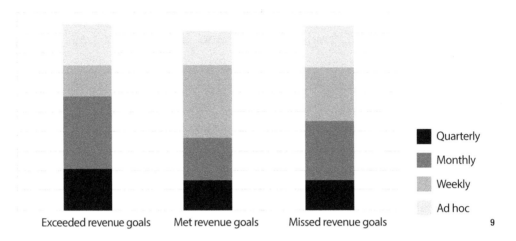

As you can see in the chart above, the cadence didn't affect the outcome. What matters is the variety of distribution and training techniques that are leveraged.

QUESTION: When a new sales tool is produced, how is it communicated to sales?

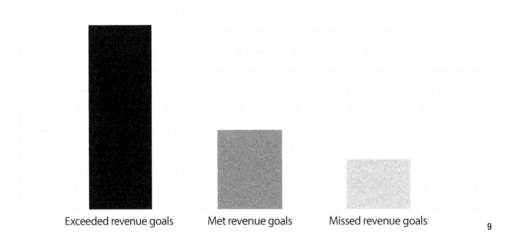

Those that exceeded revenue goals were 3.5X as likely as those that missed goals to use all available methods to communicate new sales tools to sales, including email, virtual and in-person training, and the use of a sales tool repository.

Let buyers drive your collateral strategy

If you're looking for a way to accelerate deals, I can guarantee that the answer is *never* more product collateral. If marketing is not careful, they can spend most of their time creating new collateral assets at the behest of sales. However, that time is often poorly spent. A lot of these requests are really a reflection of sales being a little lazy, rather than a lack of information from the buyer. For example, instead of modifying a sales presentation, salespeople often ask marketing to create a new one. Don't get me wrong— marketing needs feedback on the assets they produce, but it's important that feedback be focused on what's really critical to the buyer, not only to the needs of the seller.

This period of misalignment is often caused by a combination of busy marketers who feel they have no time to speak with buyers, and a resistant sales team that wants to "protect" its accounts. The result is a lack of engagement and insight. The most successful organizations have broken down this unspoken barrier between marketing and buyers, and the resulting insights have meaningful impact. Marketers at organizations who exceed revenue goals are 2X as likely to participate in customer and prospect meetings as those who miss revenue goals.[9] These top performers even go as far as to consult buyers when evaluating what sales enablement resources to build and enhance. Those who exceed revenue goals are 3.1X as likely as those who just meet revenue goals to survey buyers when evaluating sales tools, and 14X as likely as those who miss revenue goals.[9]

Use service-level agreements

A key practice of those who exceed revenue goals, one that is in stark contrast to those who meet or miss revenue goals, is documenting service-level agreements (SLAs) between sales and marketing.

Teams that perform best document more service-level agreements between sales and marketing than those that simply meet or miss revenue goals. Those that exceed revenue goals even collect data points such as win/loss data in a formalized manner. They not only agree on lead scoring criteria for sales follow-up, but on the time it should take from when a lead is assigned to when sales follows up. It's this closed-loop accountability that clearly makes a difference, as evidenced by the revenue performance of companies in my study.

Don't forget to include database integrity expectations. For example, though salespeople may complain that it takes time to document why a deal was lost in the CRM, marketing can't add the right features to the product to increase win rate if no empirical data is available. What's more, marketing can't run a competitive swap-out campaign if no one is tagged in the database as having a competitive product. The bottom line is this: administrative database work is not busywork. Marketing can't segment the database to improve campaign conversion and accelerate the pipeline without sales filling in the blanks.

CHAPTER 4

Quality vs. Quantity Leads

For a sales leader or marketing professional, nothing gets blood pumping and veins popping more than talking about lead goals. Typically, marketing does some backward math based on expected revenue contribution and industry benchmark conversion rates; all the while sales demands more leads.

This is the result of a very real quality vs. quantity battle going on between sales and marketing teams across the globe. As pressure to increase customer acquisition rises, sales teams demand more leads. Marketing responds by increasing programs that drive new names into the database, yet conversion rates and results remain stagnant. It's an exhausting cycle full of blame and finger-pointing.

Marketing thinks it delivers…

But sales perceives…

QUALITY VS. QUANTITY LEADS

Why is this the case? My explanation is simple. When marketers focus on getting "more" leads, rather than quality leads, the result is a messy mix of poor-quality leads that sales largely ignores while marketing celebrates "meeting" its lead goals.

This has gotten ugly. I remember working for an early-stage technology company. There were two of us in marketing and about a zillion things to do. We had few customers and our brand was just starting to come together. We had a beta version of our product, a big dream and a capital reserve to spend cautiously.

We spent a significant portion of our budget partnering with an outside telemarketing firm to set up meetings with chief information officers (CIOs) at large enterprises. We worked hard to provide the calling staff with an enticing story and a compelling reason for these executives to take our meeting. We were having some early success.

In our outreach program, our definition of "leads" was appointments with a buyer who met our prospect profile—CIO or VP of Enterprise Architecture, or Data Warehousing for very large, data-intensive enterprises. We'd set up dozens of meetings with our target audience, some of which had blossomed into opportunities that looked ready to beta-test our product.

I felt pretty good going into our sales and marketing review meeting. But then the all-too-familiar blame game started. The CEO began questioning the lead "source" of everyone in our pipeline. Marketing was getting no credit, and I was mad. We got into a pretty heated conversation. I left the meeting feeling devalued, frustrated and totally flustered. How could I feel so confident about what we delivered, while my counterparts felt so disappointed?

After a pint of ice cream to lick my wounds, I took a step back and tried to retrace the heart of our debate. It came down to the fact that we didn't have a shared definition of success. We both agreed on our target profile. But we weren't aligned around what really mattered and what we were looking for. We needed to flesh out deeper characteristics at each target organization that would indicate a willingness to try a yet-unproven technology. While marketing focused on setting up meetings with as many target buyers as we could, sales really only needed to talk to those who were likely to be early adopters.

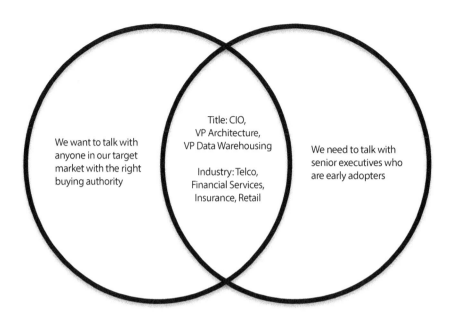

We want to talk with anyone in our target market with the right buying authority

Title: CIO, VP Architecture, VP Data Warehousing

Industry: Telco, Financial Services, Insurance, Retail

We need to talk with senior executives who are early adopters

Many of the meetings we set up did not turn into opportunities—not because we had targeted the wrong title, or the wrong company, but because we hadn't qualified the conversation to probe for early adopter propensity such as an emerging technologies team, or risk-taking personality attributes.

While the executive team had originally said they wanted *more* meetings, it turns out that's not really what they meant. What they wanted was *higher-quality* meetings that would lead to more *opportunities*.

Sadly, my story is not an isolated example. Here are some of the results of the 2016 B2B Sales & Marketing Collaboration Study,[10] where 123 survey respondents gave us a glimpse into their work experiences:

- ○ 66.9% of respondents report that sales teams are *not* rewarded for supporting marketing objectives, although most report marketing objectives align to the greater business goals.

---

10 http://marketingadvisorynetwork.com/wp-content/uploads/2016/03/Sales-and-Marketing-Collaboration-Study-June-2016.pdf

○ 57% of organizations report that fewer than 85% of leads delivered by marketing are followed up by sales (some saying that that figure is as low as 25% or less). When you consider the cost to acquire leads, this lack of follow-up not only hurts conversion rates, it also hurts in terms of cold, hard cash. For example, if your marketing team generates 5,000 leads, and sales only follows up on 85%, that leaves 750 leads going to waste. At $5, $10 or $20 per lead, that's a lot of budget misused.

The solution has been to implement lead scoring models that provide a gate to ensure appropriate engagement with prospective buyers.

The problem is, most organizations build lead scoring models incorrectly by assuming the more someone engages with us, the better-quality lead they have become. Every part of me says that cumulative lead scoring that assigns points based on individual actions over time (such as a content download) are logical. The more activity a lead takes with my company, the more interested they must be in my offering, right? Although logical, it is just not true.

If we look at the pattern behind every complex buying process, it's evident that the people who interact with your company do so at one of several stages of readiness. Early-stage buyers are still examining their potential issues, likely unaware they even have a problem worth solving yet, and are certainly not ready to discuss your products. Middle and late-stage buyers have identified that, yes, there's an issue they need to fix, and they may be in the process of identifying vendors to provide a solution. Each interaction a prospect takes with your content and your team falls into one of these stages, and marketers must score leads appropriately. Someone may interact with you time and time again, but not be anywhere close to buying as they completely fall outside your target criteria. Conversely, a very hot lead may only interact with you once. This trips up many of the most well-intentioned lead scoring strategies.

After attempting to implement cumulative lead scoring systems for three organizations I finally realized that, despite gut instinct, what really matters is the last interaction you had with a buyer. Marketers should build propensity-to-buy models based on the most current interaction you have with each individual, and align this to your buyer personas. Let's look at a practical example.

Gerry Atric signs up for every web seminar. He's an independent consultant with a very small customer base. His current practice complements your offering, but he does not resell your solution and never will. Using a traditional cumulative scoring model, Gerry Atric is likely to accumulate a lot of points and bubble up as a hot lead when in reality he's not someone your salespeople will get value in contacting. Does that mean you don't want him to attend a web seminar? No, of course not. You just don't want him to be rolled up to the sales team as a hot lead.

Now let's look at Jack Flash. Jack has not visited your website before, but he did download a whitepaper entitled "Selecting the Right Vendor." Under traditional cumulative scoring models Jack would score very low. He's never exhibited any activity before and only recently accessed one whitepaper. But the topic of the whitepaper is very telling. It is targeted toward people in an active purchasing process. What else do you know about Jack besides this action? If he has "student" in his title, he is not a hot lead unless you are in the education business. If Jack was in your database as a target for the sales team based on his role, now that's a potentially hot lead that should be flagged for sales follow-up because the content accessed indicated buying readiness.

CASE STUDY: LESS IS MORE. HOW WE REDUCED QUANTITY TO IMPROVE QUALITY AND DRIVE REVENUE GROWTH

The CEO and VP of sales for a $20 million technology business had just hired me to build a marketing plan that would increase the number of leads being produced.

The Problem

The company's VP of marketing had left the company a couple of weeks before I was invited to consult, yet the organization was still held to aggressive growth plans set by its board. Sales said they needed more leads to fuel the customer acquisition needed to meet these goals, and that the current crop of leads from marketing simply weren't making the cut.

The Situation

The request was clear: "We need more leads!" However, the real mission was to grow the business, and this required something quite different. This company's marketing was producing plenty of volume; the problem was quality. Leads simply weren't converting.

The Research

I teamed up with sales operations and the marketing team to dig into the current lead management systems to examine *where* leads had come from, *what* actions they had taken previously, and *how* well they converted once they were passed to sales for follow-up. I also sought to understand what agreements, if any, were in place between marketing and sales to make this transition a smooth one.

I found that, in the hope of hitting high-level and misinformed "lead goals," marketing was sending every contact that exhibited any activity to sales. Once there, salespeople felt their time spent on follow-up activity was wasted on leads who weren't ready to consider their solution. This led to a sense of mistrust between the two departments— sales felt marketing wasn't providing useful fuel for growth, and marketing felt sales was simply ignoring the results of their efforts.

The Solution

Imagine walking into a meeting with the CEO and head of sales and telling them that not only were we *not* going to increase the volume of leads produced, we were going to significantly *cut* the volume of leads passed to sales. They almost fell out of their chairs as they stared at me in disbelief. Secretly I think they were looking for the hidden camera, convinced I had to be pranking them. When the shock wore off I stepped them through what I had discovered.

From my research efforts, I was able to examine and segment leads produced from the previous few months. I put them into one of four categories:

1. **Suspects** were new names added to the database but with almost no meaningful contact with the organization. These names came from targeted list purchases or trade show attendee lists where the company had exhibited. These contacts had never visited the organization, so were not even yet leads, but rather Suspects. They matched the profile criteria of contacts who might benefit from their solution but lacked enough meaningful interaction for a salesperson to be in contact with them. This segment in particular had grown in size over the past

couple of quarters because marketing was under a lot of pressure to produce more leads.

2. **Qualified Leads** had downloaded product-related information and industry reports, registered for a web seminar, or visited the company's booth at a trade show. This activity would indicate they were in the right state of mind to speak to a salesperson to further qualify the opportunity. I was very intentional about using the word *qualified*, since it was meant to help sales immediately understand that these leads were not the same as the suspects they had been given previously. Qualified Leads who accessed buying-oriented content (such as a request for proposal (RFP) template) were especially flagged as urgent.

3. **Inbound Qualified Leads** were those contacts that had come to our organization proactively. Segmenting this category of leads introduced the notion of hand-raisers to the organization. These Inbound Qualified Leads went immediately to sales for action because they exhibited the most clear behavior to indicate a propensity to buy. To qualify for this category, the prospect had to fill out a request for quote, request for demo, download trial software, or complete a "contact me" form or indicate they had an active project in process on any of our other registration forms.

4. We also introduced **Referral Leads**, introductions that came directly from partners or other clients.

Our baseline report showed that almost 60% of the "leads" previously produced were really Suspects and that Inbound Qualified Leads were virtually nonexistent.

Lead Type	Baseline
Suspect	59.8%
Qualified Lead	38.6%
In-Bound	1.6%
Referral	0%

After our effort to properly segment and qualify contacts, I knew that getting leadership on the same page about the purpose and goals of marketing was the only way this project would have lasting effects internally. I ensured that sales leadership, the marketing team, and our C-level stakeholders agreed and understood that Suspects would *not* be included against the overall lead count. We also agreed that rather than grow lead volume, the company would need to focus on lead quality.

Further, we agreed to tag these Qualified Leads for action within the company's CRM system. To ensure that sales would follow up with qualified leads appropriately, we set in place a service-level agreement (SLA) that clearly set forth the expectations from both parties—sales and marketing. What's more, that SLA was championed and sponsored by a C-level stakeholder. When the SLA was not met, the lead was reassigned to a different salesperson.

The Results

In the end we cut the number of leads produced by 50% but the quality increased significantly. In addition to revenue growth, we saw the length of time between buying stages decrease and a more healthy relationship develop between sales and marketing. It wasn't uncommon for sales representatives to stop me in the hallway and remark that the leads they now received were of much better quality.

Lead Type	Baseline	6-Months Later
Suspect	59.8%	0%
Qualified Lead	38.6%	89.1%
In-Bound	1.6%	9.5%
Referral	0%	1.4%

50% Lead Count

25% Revenue Growth

This team deserves a great deal of credit, because it took a lot of trust to make an adjustment this big, and it involved multiple team members. In the end, however, it paid off in spades. Sales and marketing had a much smoother working relationship. Leads that were passed to sales were held accountable to SLAs with pride. And most important, revenue grew 25% without increasing the marketing budget.

By changing what we measured and how we scored leads for sales assignment, we changed the behavior of this organization to focus on the right set of activities aligned to the right people, rather than focusing on volume.

HOW-TO GUIDELINES: LEAD SCORING

In this chapter I hope we've put an end to the quality vs. quantity lead debate and you are now ready to build a lead scoring framework that *scales growth, not lead volume*.

My experience across organizations has uncovered four essential factors in every high-performing lead scoring system that delivers both quality and growth (not to mention happy sales teams):

1. Score based on buyer signals, not volume.

Buyer readiness should be at the heart of your lead scoring model. It's the *nature* of the action, not its frequency that indicates when sales should engage. Sales should receive "leads" at the moment buyers take buying signal actions, including:

- Requesting contact
- Requesting quote
- Requesting demo
- Registering for evaluation or trial version of your product
- Accessing tangible buying interest content such as ROI calculators, buyer's guide, vendor comparisons, or RFP templates

2. Don't become too dependent on automation.

Is the information you are supplying accurate? Do you have a valid email address and phone number? Is the client in a geography you serve? Does the title of the lead resonate with your solution's selling model?

Marketing automation systems have advanced so much in the last five years that it's tempting to automate every part of our lead scoring environment. While there is great value in using technology to manage our lead distribution processes, no system is fail-proof. I can't tell you the number of "Mickey Mouse," "System Admin," or "Junk Mail" so-called leads that make it through automated systems. They appear to pass all the necessary criteria. They have a first and last name, valid email address, and have participated in the appropriate programs. The only problem—Mickey Mouse, System Admin, and Junk Mail are all people trying hard to hide their real identity.

QUALITY VS. QUANTITY LEADS

When sales receive these contacts tagged as leads they lose faith in the system. Conversely, some really hot leads never make it past the threshold of automated systems. How many times have you met a key buyer at a trade show, scanned their badge, and then proceeded to have a lengthy conversation, only to determine they are a hot prospect? How often do you actually remember to tag them in the scanning system as hot? How often do you think your sales peers do the same? Or are they relying on a business card exchange to get the job done? Let's face it—no matter how good your system, leaving all the work to automated programming is error prone. A regular dose of good old-fashioned eyeballing goes a long way.

Automation and quality tools have dramatically improved database integrity, but they can't apply human intuition. The following manual processes are worth following to optimize your data quality even when good automation processes are in place.

- Before uploading a list to your database give it a manual once-over. Select a random handful of records and look up the person in LinkedIn, ZoomInfo or Hoovers. Does the data match?

- Check your new leads queue once a week. Look for leads that sales has not converted. Can you tell by looking at them that the data is of poor quality? Are you seeing the same name appear eight times in a row? How many people with titles you don't target are you seeing?

- At least four times a year, do a total database assessment. Use the same techniques you use to check individual records—only this time, scan across your entire database. You'll be shocked to learn how much your database has degraded over time.

- Trust your common sense. Do you think Jon Smith from ABC Company in Denver is the same person as Johnny Smith from ABC Company in Colorado? I bet they are, even if they have slightly different email addresses. You have common sense—it's OK to rely on it. Go ahead, merge the records.

- Welcome feedback from salespeople who are calling into your leads day after day. Open a channel of manageable communication by having monthly feedback sessions or even weekly check-ins. Your counterparts on the front lines are full of valuable insight.

In Chapter 12, "Data, Meet Human", we explore additional data best practices.

3. Be transparent.

Trigger-based lead scoring does not mean you should hide all action by a contact. It just means you restrict assigning tasks for sales until there are agreed-upon actions taken by the contact. All actions such as content downloads or website visits should be noted in your sales force automation system. If sales is browsing, this will allow them to put any future conversations in context for the buyer.

In addition to contact-specific triggers, it is worth experimenting with account-level thresholds. Low-level activity happening across a large number of contacts at the same company could signal buying intent. While these should be treated differently from other triggers, flagging these accounts can provide valuable insights for both sales and marketing, since strategic account teams seek clues about when a company is ready to engage.

4. Adjust program activity to match trigger model.

When you report on leads it's important to emphasize conversion rates, not just the end value of each lead. Consider the sample below as a way to frame your evaluation of specific activities.

- ❍ Assess conversion rates-to-close by type of activity
- ❍ Reallocate dollars toward high deal-conversion metrics
- ❍ Focus demand-generation efforts on all parts of the buyer's journey, not just problem identification

Original Lead Source	Days to Demo	Days to Close	Close %	# Touches to Close	Revenue Influenced
Trade show	24	180	10%	23	$$$$
Pay Per Click	98	220	1%	25	$
Web seminar-product	5	64	28%	14	$$$
Web seminar-industry	22	56	17%	37	$$$
Request for quote	2	14	65%	6	$$$$
Whitepaper download	12	78	9%	39	$$
Product whitepaper	7	22	12%	10	$$$$
Eval download	2	31	75%	5	$$$$$

HOW-TO GUIDELINES: DRIVING ORGANIZATIONAL CHANGE

When you take all these factors into consideration you realize quickly that "more" can't be manufactured right away. It takes time to build relationships, uncover prospects in the later stages of their buying process, and develop compelling content to nurture Suspects into Qualified Leads. The truth is, time often isn't on your side when the Quantity Heavyweight Champion is breathing down your neck asking for a match after every quarterly sales meeting.

Here are a few tips to help your organization transition from one that values volume to one that values quality.

1. Set expectations.

How long will it take to feel the impact of quality lead program management? In my experience, it takes about two to three full sales cycles for the program to fully mature. If your sales cycle from quality lead to close is an average of 90 days, expect 6–9 months for a nurture program to have significant measurable impact. Set milestones along the way so the team can understand how you are progressing against that goal.

2. Find quick wins.

Two to three sales cycles is a long time to wait for results. Most organizations aren't that patient. Instead of giving up, find quick wins that can be produced and promoted in the beginning of your program. Run a pipeline acceleration promotion to progress the hottest deals targeted at late-stage leads. Spotlight inbound wins (even if there are only small numbers) to showcase the power of nurturing. Celebrate a sales rep's particularly good use of the program with broad public recognition. The bottom line is, marketers must do whatever it takes to keep momentum and show progress against long-term goals. Remember, patience is a virtue when driving organizational change, but perception is reality.

3. Have faith.

As marketers we know that nurturing buyer relationships is essential. We've read the research, we've experimented with organizations in the past, we've built lead scoring models. Yet after a few bursts of impatience by the organization at large, even our most steadfast confidence can be shaken. Are we doing the right thing? Should we just buy another list? Maybe I should loosen lead accuracy criteria just a little bit to meet my numbers? I understand the temptation—but *don't* lose faith. Give yourself and the team time to work out the kinks, give buyers time to mature their relationship with you and hang on to the end goal of quality.

4. Take everyone on the journey.

What has become second nature to marketers isn't always natural for the rest of the organization. A regular cadence of education and internal communication programs is critical to keep your team and your constituents engaged and supportive of your initiatives. Once people understand and buy into the quality-vs.-quantity debate, they'll start to throw punches right alongside you. Run workshops, have lunchtime huddles, share research—all of this will compel the organization to be in the same corner.

5. Last, don't set it and forget it.

After weeks of hard work, you rolled out a trigger-based lead system. If you were wise, you avoided the temptation to set your lead scoring model to match your lead goal. I know it is tempting to set criteria to ensure that you hit the volume commitments your sales executives have requested, but I hope you didn't fall into that trap.

Instead, you built the model on what you think drives conversions. You have agreed to follow-up SLAs between sales and marketing and everything is off to a good start. After a couple of months of monitoring, the excitement of something new wears off and you're sucked into the next major initiative. The problem is, the market has shifted, buyer behavior has changed, and the lead triggers you identified in the first rollout have become stale and now don't account for the new content or learning you've made along the way.

When undergoing lead scoring and management improvements, it is important that you don't just set it and forget it. Instead, regularly survey sales to determine how well the lead scoring system reflects the reality of buyers. Run conversion reports to determine if hot leads truly convert better than other lead categories. Explore which buyer actions lead to larger sales. And do it every 3–6 months depending on your sales cycle. Then, rinse and repeat.

CHAPTER 5

Stop Chasing the C-Suite

A client and I were chatting over steamy hot chocolate and scones (yes, I have the best meetings) when suddenly this Director of Demand Generation turned very serious. I could see her body tense as she asked, "So, how can we get to the C-suite? Our executive team is very frustrated that Chief Information Officers don't want to meet with us. We planned an executive summit for CIOs, and only three people registered." In response, I couldn't help but ask, "Why do you feel getting to the CIO is important?"

You see, this company sold technology, but rather than sell to the CIO, they sold it to operational leaders and their IT manager counterparts. These managers had been buying, using and advocating for their product for years.

The conversation went like this:

ME: *Why does the team want to attract the CIO?*

CLIENT: *To be honest, I don't think we need to focus on them but the executive team is pushing very hard.*

ME: *Why do you think they are pushing so hard?*

CLIENT: *They think we have to be on the mind of the CIO or else we haven't "made it."*

ME: *What do they hope to result from a meeting with the CIO?*

CLIENT: *It will make everyone feel good. They think because we sell technology, we just have to be on the radar of the CIO. Oh, and somehow it will shorten the sales cycle, increase deal size, and make us more profitable.*

The rest of the conversation continued in the same vein. Unfortunately, this client's management team had fallen into the same trap as so many businesses before them. The allure of being on the C-suite's agenda is tantalizing. We believe it will magically remove barriers to the sales process.

This same scenario and conversation has played out time and time again across many of my clients, and within organizations where I've been employed full-time. The urgent importance of the elusive C-level executive to marketing and sales is a pervasive misconception that leads to wasted time, effort and money.

The truth is, chasing the C-suite can waste enormous amounts of money and energy when these executives don't consider your solution a priority. Studies show that 81% of non-C-suite employees influence purchase decisions.[11] In fact, the average B2B decision-making group includes 5.4 buyers.[12] Yet many marketers end up chasing leads that won't drive significant business and will have little or no impact on the sales cycle. In my experience, programs involved with targeting members of the C-suite have cost anywhere from 10 to 20X more than those targeting less senior, but still influential buyers.

Don't get me wrong—there are some companies where selling to a three-letter title that starts with C makes sense. But in my experience, the other 97% of marketing teams waste time and money chasing after executives who simply don't need—or want—to learn about their offer. It doesn't matter if your CXO target is a CIO, CFO, CMO or CEO. Perhaps it's one of the trendy new C-level titles like Chief Revenue of Chief Customer Officer. Chasing any C-suite employee costs a lot of money and effort.

---

11 Google, https://www.thinkwithgoogle.com/articles/the-changing-face-b2b-marketing.html

12 https://www.cebglobal.com/marketing-communications/mobilizer.html

The next time you, or your boss, is tempted to chase the C-suite, ask these four important questions to determine if the effort is worthwhile:

1. Is the C-suite the only title that has authority to purchase your product? If so, does the cost of your solution represent at least 5% of their total budget?

2. Is your offering going to drive strategic value to the organization beyond a single line of business or function?

3. Is one of the C-suite buyer's top 3 priorities a problem your offering can address?

4. Will promoting your solution to the organization advance the career or credibility of the C-suite executive?

If you can't answer yes to these questions, you are better off spending marketing dollars focused on your real buyer. The persona research you will read about in Chapter 10 will uncover details about these real buyers. Stop chasing the elusive CXO who really doesn't care about your offering, and instead arm your champion with the tools they need to successfully build consensus internally, justify the change in their organization, and ultimately make a purchase.

If after answering these questions you decide going after the CXO is critical; spend time to build a nurturing program that is sensitive to their unique demands and be prepared to invest proportionally. I detail some how-to guidelines later in this chapter.

CASE STUDY: LOOK INTO MY EYES...

The situation

Sometimes I imagine C-level executives saying, "Look into my eyes. My CXO greatness will hypnotize you..."

As marketing and sales professionals, we sometimes get caught up in the allure of "selling up" even when the need doesn't really exist. That's exactly what happened to this software company that serves the manufacturing industry.

For 10 years this business had benefited from steady growth and become a leader in their field. They boasted many name-brand clients, and hundreds of professionals joined them each year for their annual conference.

The problem

In the previous 18 months, growth had stagnated. They seemed to have hit a wall and the sales team was not hitting their new revenue targets despite an overhaul in sales leadership. They opted to dramatically cut marketing staff and double down on reaching the C-level audience. Their theory was, if they could get the attention of the CIO, they could upsell more services to their target buyer community, and reduce the length of the sales process by seeking senior approval up front.

The attempted solution

With good intentions, the newly diminished marketing team set out to fill the pipeline with CIO meetings. They hired a professional agency to design a direct mail program. They invested $35,000, and from start to execution the program took three months to develop, and ran for 30 days.

The program consisted of:

- Direct mail — 365 direct mail letters were sent, containing a basic introduction to the issues addressed by the vendor, along with an offer to conduct a complimentary process assessment that would compare the organization to industry standards. The assessment was given an expiration date of one month.

- Follow-up email and telemarketing — Two email follow-up messages were sent, along with outbound calls to everyone on the recipient list. In addition, emails were sent to a broader list of executives, in hopes that they might be familiar with the vendor in case the CIO asked about the communication.

On the surface, this sounds like a reasonable program—until you look at the results.

The results

The results were a devastating disappointment. Zero meetings. Yes—zero meetings! No click-through on the emails, and only one was forwarded to a peer. Feedback from the calling team indicated that in most cases the executive's administrator received the mail and email and it had not been shared with the targeted recipient. They didn't recognize the company name and nothing in the communications felt urgent to them. In the rare case they were able to speak with the executive, they were told the targeted buyer was not interested or was already doing an assessment with a different firm.

Luckily, in parallel, the company started experimenting with different types of content, targeting the operations leaders who represented their additional buyers. The content wasn't dramatically different, but the formats were new—infographics, checklists, 3–4-page issue briefs. As a result of these efforts, email open-rates and content downloads increased steadily, putting more leads into the system for sales follow-up. These buyers were not CXOs, but they had budget authority and the sales team knew exactly how to leverage them to push forward an opportunity.

Lessons learned

For this organization, the CIO was not their target buyer. By trying to force an unnatural match a lot of time was wasted.

Here's what went wrong:

- No one talked to CIOs ahead of the campaign. If they had, they would have realized that, although this company's offerings provided value to their clients, it did nothing to address the strategic agenda of the CIO. It did, however, align with the needs of their colleagues in operations.
- They were smart to invest in direct mail, but their offer was not compelling. CIOs simply didn't want a discovery engagement with a company they did not trust.
- They failed to invest in direct mail that would stand out. A simple letter is easily lost, and the offer looked like several that crossed the CIO's desk every day.

At the end of this campaign, $35,000 and four months were spent chasing an audience they didn't need to engage and who didn't have interest in talking to them. Imagine if that money, wasted on irrelevant C-suite targets, was instead spent enhancing their outreach and booking meetings with lead targets that truly resonated.

HOW-TO GUIDELINES: ATTRACT THE C-SUITE

In appropriate scenarios, attracting C-suite buyers is in fact a necessary action. It can be done, but batten down the hatches and get ready for a bumpy ride. In this section we will explore a series of guidelines you should follow for minimizing resource drain and maximizing results when targeting the C-suite.

1. Be *very* targeted. C-suite marketing is not a volume game.

You must not only focus on the buyer's title, but also ensure that the organization they serve aligns to your offering. Verify the location, size and industry of your targeted contacts and, if possible, any other characteristic that might indicate a propensity to buy. For example, one provider I work with was targeting CMOs with their e-commerce conversion solution. In order to justify their solution, they knew customers needed a minimum traffic threshold of one million visitors per month. To determine if the prospective buyer met that threshold, they used a free online traffic estimator to verify their targeted accounts' monthly web traffic.

2. Forget email. Get your physical mailing address list ready.

C-level contacts are not going to respond to cold email outreach, period. You may occasionally get a lucky response, but hinging the success of a program on email alone is a waste of your time.

Email by itself is a poor outreach mechanism for C-level contacts because:

- They have some of the busiest email inboxes at their company due to the nature of their role.
- C-level staff frequently have email gatekeepers who delete unsolicited email before it ever reaches its intended audience.
- C-level names and email addresses are generally easy to find, so everyone tries to email them, further flooding their inbox and creating a crowded space for you to break through.

Use email only as a secondary, follow-up outreach mechanism. Instead, consider dimensional direct mail offers that relate to your value proposition and send it via Priority Mail to ensure that it gets delivered.

Here are several examples of very different approaches I've seen succeed in supporting meeting acquisition campaigns to the C-suite:

1. Personalized competitive analysis comparing their organization to a benchmark of competitors, delivered in a padded envelope.
2. Video "cards" that play a personalized video when opened

3. A small box filled with LEGO pieces that featured a custom piece with the company's logo on it. (Don't worry—it's not nearly as hard to pull off as you think! Stickers are an amazing thing.)

Although very different, all three of these approaches shares one thing in common—they stand out from the everyday mail that piles up on your prospect's desk.

Two other really important things to remember when designing your direct mail program.

1. Direct mail programs are expensive. You should test programs in small batches, 50–100 at a time, before investing too much money.

2. Don't expect a *lot* of inbound response to even the most clever campaign. Your goal is to be memorable so that when you reach out after receipt, your prospect will remember your offer and brand.

3. Remember: Substance over style.

As you are developing your program, don't get too excited about the delivery format. That's the fun part, but the important part is your offer and value proposition. Relevancy for your specific audience is essential. You must not only catch their attention, you have to keep it. Insights from your persona research can uncover exactly what buttons to press and what critical issues are top-of-mind for your buyer. Whether you're offering an assessment, free research, or exclusive event, make sure your offer is relevant to their role.

As an extension of this rule of thumb, please don't try to bribe your recipients. When I worked at an accounting solution firm, we once ran a campaign to CFOs that offered a very expensive golf club in exchange for responding. We planned for the sales team to deliver the golf clubs in person and hence secure the meeting. Well, we did get a decent amount of response, but no one wanted to talk about our offering. In fact, when they realized we would hand-deliver the club, many declined the offer to which they had responded. They were in the market for a new golf club. It's too bad we sold accounting software.

4. Know how to get past the gatekeeper.

C-level staffers have gatekeepers who are very good at their job. If you want to get past them, you better have a compelling reason for them to pass you along to the boss.

Telling them you have a great product their supervisor is going to love is not compelling. You have to explain in terms a non-domain expert is going to recognize as urgent. For example, your first introduction into the company should not focus on what you sell, but rather a challenge or problem the company experiences. If the company has interacted with any of your marketing material before, that's excellent fodder to demonstrate to the gatekeeper that there has been some previous interaction that warrants a follow-up. Arm sales with this history to help them demonstrate that they understand the business of their prospect (and their gatekeeper).

5. Partner with someone.

If you don't have existing relationships with the contacts you hope to target, find a relationship that does exist.

- ○ Is there another, complementary vendor with whom you do business you can leverage? I've often partnered with another vendor to conduct joint research or cosponsor an exclusive, invitation-only executive event.

- ○ Can you leverage an existing customer relationship? I've often created intimate dinner events where clients are comfortable inviting their peers to join them for a night of networking and good food. While you won't talk a lot about your solution at these dinners, you will begin to bond with your target audience.

- ○ You can also leverage interesting work from your existing customer relationships to attract an audience. For example, at one organization, the Cleveland Indians were a happy customer. Baseball was a fun draw for our audience, and we knew we could create a VIP experience the local market would value. With the support of our customer advocate at the Cleveland Indians, we booked a suite at an evening game and hosted an evening of fun and learning. Of course, being from Boston, I picked a game against the Red Sox so we'd feel a win no matter what! Although the guest host was there on our behalf, they discussed not only their environment as it related to our business, but the overall needs of their organization. Our tech-savvy audience was thrilled with this inside look at the business of baseball—it gave them a new way of considering our solution in the context of a real-world example with which they could each relate. The draw may have been baseball, but each guest left the event with a new perspective on our company and its value. We even delighted them further with access to batting practice and some special autograph signing. It's a night I won't soon forget, and neither did our guests.

Note: You don't need to have Major League Baseball clients to host an exciting evening. I've set up similar events at manufacturing facilities and even offices with an interesting view. Know your audience and plan accordingly.

○ If finding one of your customers to agree to act as host is challenging, consider hiring an association or publication to design an event. Though they come with a cost, trade publications do a good job of using editorial relationships to host roundtable discussions around topics that are near and dear to your customers. The forums are intimate environments where your executives can establish themselves as thought leaders and valuable contributors to the community. While expensive, these publications can be used to target buyers that don't yet know you or your work.

6. Develop compelling thought leadership assets.

Unless all the stars and moons align around you, asking a C-level prospect to meet with you to discuss their environment or see a demo of your solutions is simply not a good door opener. You have to build trust before asking for these types of meetings.

To build this trust, offer your audience compelling new research or insight they might not get anywhere else. Some ways to implement this include fielding a survey to your market segment and publishing the anonymized results as a benchmark. You may also have data in your product usage that could yield interesting trends when looked at in aggregate. Your founder or executive team likely has deep industry knowledge and a fresh point of view for the future of your space. Every successful company has valuable domain knowledge, a unique perspective, and proprietary insight somewhere within your organization. Tap into that resource and take the time to package this information in a compelling fashion. Save the hard sell for another time.

7. Build champions.

The most effective way to reach a C-level executive is for someone on their team to schedule a meeting on your behalf. While that isn't always possible, it's worth investing in a champion relationship because they can provide insight that will help you impress the CXO, along with introductions. To make this work, it's important that marketing and sales partner together to identify potential champions, then articulate what questions you want them to answer.

This is an extremely effective method but it takes some endurance. Don't expect to call up a potential champion and get what you need in a single conversation—instead, approach your relationship to this individual as a partnership in which you'll help and guide them to make the business case for your solution. Ultimately, your job is to promote and support their individual goals within their organization. That's what turns a prospect into a champion.

CHAPTER 6

Account Based Marketing (It's Not What You Think)

Marketers love to brainstorm with one another about our work because it allows us the chance to figure out solutions from new perspectives. I recently had lunch with a friend of mine who works as a demand generation marketer. As in many of our past conversations, we celebrated recent achievements and commiserated over what hadn't worked out. On this particular day, my friend lamented that her recent Account Based Marketing (ABM) program had failed. I was curious about what she had executed, and asked for more details.

My friend described a content syndication program where a whitepaper was distributed to contacts at specific companies. Trying my best not to lead an inquisition, I asked a few follow-up questions.

1. What was the profile of the contacts you were reaching out to? *"Fortune 2000 companies. Large companies have a need for our technology."*

2. Was the content personalized in any way to the companies being served? *"No. We used an existing whitepaper. Everyone received the same content."*

3. How were "leads" followed up? *"The sales team called every contact and tried to set up a meeting. Many of the contacts were not interested in our core value proposition."*

4. How were the target companies selected? *"We limited it to Fortune 2000 companies because they are the right size."*

5. How did you measure the program? *"The sales team rejected many of the leads that we generated. In addition we converted fewer of these leads to demonstrations than we do with our cold-call lists."*

I realized that, while there is nothing wrong with leveraging existing content to target a segment of the market, the program wasn't actually an Account Based Marketing program at all. What my friend described was a content syndication program targeting a limited universe of companies. The distinction is subtle but very important. At its core, failure to treat the program as a true ABM initiative was the primary problem.

Defining Account Based Marketing

Account Based Marketing is the discipline of directing marketing programs at a dedicated set of accounts. It flips our orientation so we focus not on an individual's action, or inaction, but look holistically at the account. One of the most common misperceptions about ABM is what constitutes an effective program. It takes more than simply using the same tactic we've always used on a more focused list of accounts: it takes tight integration with sales.

ABM requires:

1. Deep analysis of accounts to identify targets with a high propensity to purchase. This means going beyond surface segmentation like company size or vertical, and looking for buying signals such as installed technologies, business actions that would indicate need and previous interactions with your organization.

2. Multi-person nurture strategies. Account Based Marketing does not ignore individuals, but rather it engages with specific contacts in the context of the organization they serve. Programs should include targeted offers intended for individuals, with consideration to the role they play within the account's buying committee. Content must be relevant to the organizations you are targeting. Effective ABM programs don't take a one-message-fits-all approach, sending the same message to all target accounts. They use the information you've collected about your account list to segment offers and content appropriately.

3. Focus on the long game. ABM is ideal for complex, long-term deals that require multiple stakeholders. For that reason, it takes time before you will see results. When considering ABM, remember that it's not about acquiring or engaging with

a single "lead" but rather about overall account penetration. Measuring success by a single tactic will lead to subpar results.

Though it may seem like a lot of work, Account Based Marketing efforts are worthwhile when focused and executed appropriately. For example, you can likely expect more efficient collaboration with sales who are oriented around target accounts, not contacts. Deal sizes tend to be larger with ABM efforts, as found in a study by Demandbase where the average contract value (ACV) for targeted accounts was 40% higher for mid-market and 35% higher for enterprise accounts.[13] Finally, it's worth noting that Account Based Marketing was found to deliver a higher ROI than any other marketing tactic by 84% of respondents to an ITSMA survey.[14]

Is ABM Right for Your Business?

Establishing a comprehensive Account Based Marketing program is going to take resources, time, and effort, so it's important to evaluate your business model to make sure it is a good fit.

These five questions will help you assess whether ABM is right for your business. You will want to account for the purchasing process, triggers, your value proposition and your organization's propensity for change.

1. Decision by committee: Is more than one person involved in purchasing your product or service? Are they spread across different functional areas? The more complex the decision process, the more value an account-based approach can provide.

2. Is a business or personal pain going to trigger a purchase of your offering? If organizational triggers are your primary driver, an account-based approach will be most effective. If an individual's pain will lead to an impulse purchase, an account-based program will be inefficient.

3. Is your value proposition easy to explain to more than the primary user of your product or service? Have you found a way to articulate your value proposition to

---

13 http://www.slideshare.net/Demandbase/3-driving-results-through-the-funnel
14 http://www.itsma.com/research/step-step-guide-abm-pitfalls-avoid-along-way/

stakeholders across the organization? If not, you are not prepared to address the broader audience within your target accounts. Don't set yourself up for failure, but rather invest resources in understanding your targets better.

4. Is your organization willing to change the core role of a "lead" and how you respond to it? ABM programs require a new way of scoring leads and assigning sales actions, one that is dependent on an account's activity as a collective unit.

5. What's the length of the buying process? ABM programs are well matched to complex buying processes where building relationships over time are important. If your sales cycle is measured in terms of days, a full ABM program may be more than you need. If, on the other hand, your average sales cycle takes weeks or months, building a system to measure and drive account activity over time is well worth the effort.

Account Based Marketing does not have to take an all-or-nothing approach. You may assign some parts of your business to follow this model, while others adopt a more traditional contact-based strategy. For example, your enterprise sales team might find ABM an effective approach, but your SMB or entry-level product may not be suited for the model.

CASE STUDY: DRIVING 3X MORE OPPORTUNITIES WITH ACCOUNT BASED MARKETING

The Challenge

Founded in 2008, and fueled by $60 million in capital, Invoca helps the modern marketer optimize for the most important step in the customer journey: the phone call. Powering more than 100 million calls per day, Invoca's Call Intelligence platform gives marketers granular campaign attribution data to understand why customers are calling, gain real-time intelligence about who's calling and analyze what's being said in conversations.

Over the years, Invoca had grown largely through efforts directed at small businesses. Bolstered by success with a small number of large clients, and a desire to accelerate revenue growth, in 2015 the company sought to expand significantly into larger enterprise businesses.

The opportunity was exciting but also arduous. In this new segment, they had to find and influence multiple buyer roles within each targeted account, and because profitability was a goal, they had to do it without applying additional marketing dollars. Spending more on existing tactics wasn't an option.

It was a challenge Julia Stead, Director of Demand Generation, and her team were anxious to solve but it required a totally new approach.

The Solution

Invoca's marketing and sales teams embarked on the company's first Account Based Marketing program. Their effort included four essential elements, all of which were built in collaboration between these two groups:

1. Account selection
2. Contact development
3. Multi-touch, cross-platform nurture programs
4. New measurement metrics

Step 1: Account selection

The hardest part of any Account Based Marketing program is identifying accounts with the highest propensity to purchase your products or services. This proved true at Invoca, which used a multi-stage process to get it right. The first step was to build an ideal customer profile (ICP). Some attributes like industry, geographic location and company size were easy to agree on and segment on. However, more meaningful but difficult-to-collect criteria were also required. Invoca knew that their offering added the most value to organizations that have high consideration purchase decisions that drive phone conversations. Industry is one factor, but not specific enough on its own. They sought additional signals by looking at what technologies were used within their target accounts, and how much digital advertising spend the company was making.

Once the ideal customer profile was identified, the team used third-party tools such as BuiltWith, Datanyze, DataFox and InsideView to acquire a list of targeted accounts that matched the profile. The initial goal was to identify 300 accounts per salesperson prioritized into three tiers, although later the team would learn that number was too large to drive deep sales engagement with each account. They moved to a model where each salesperson focused on 25 accounts supported by heavy marketing investment, and marketing identified and nurtured an additional 75. In this plan, sales action was only initiated when the prospect responded to campaign tactics by raising their hand.

The team took an important next step and shared the lists with the sales team for manual review and augmentation. Upon completion, marketing used a predictive analytics engine, Everstring, to score the existing database against the ideal profile. Existing data was somewhat limited and they found the predictive model left a significant gap in contact coverage in targeted accounts. The team purchased data to fill the gaps where available, and encouraged sales to play an active role in filling out missing data points through phone discovery and social search programs.

Step 2: Contact discovery

For contact selection, the sales team used tools like LinkedIn and Datanyze to import the right profile target contacts into the database. They also did a lot of manual research and discovery via social media and third-party tools, and used phone conversations to verify the quality of the contact data.

Step 3: Multi-touch, cross-platform nurture programs

Armed with targeted new data, the team audited existing marketing programs to redirect resources from generalized programs to focus on targeted accounts. While they did not eliminate all traditional channels, dollars were reallocated toward more focused efforts. For example, trade show schedules were evaluated for alignment with target accounts, and pre-show meeting acquisition programs were given priority over flashy booth space.

A major driver of efficiency in this effort was to direct most display advertising toward targeted accounts, excluding ads to accounts that did not match their ideal customer profile. They used Terminus (integrated with Salesforce.com) to facilitate the process.

In addition, the team sought to attract and nurture accounts across all touchpoints, including events, email and direct mail. Marketo was used to coordinate a sophisticated, multi-stage, trigger-based nurture programs. For example, one program started with an educational blog post. If a contact read the blog post, a case study was served up in both video and written format. If the contact clicked through and watched at least one minute of the video, they were fast-tracked with an incentivized demo request, which would schedule a 30-minute demo in exchange for an Amazon gift card. The goal of the program was to match the tempo of communications to the level of contact engagement. But Invoca's strategy didn't stop at the contact level, as a traditional marketing program would. In their account-based model, they evaluated a contact's actions against other contacts at the same account. For example, when a demo was booked and an opportunity created, demo marketing was paused to the other individuals in their organization. Invoca's marketing team knew sales was working hard to make sure multiple contacts were engaged in the meeting, so they let sales' engagement lead that effort so as not to overwhelm the buyers.

Step 4: New measurement metrics

Underpinning all of this was a new approach to measure marketing. Invoca threw out the old model of tracking lead volume, MQL and SQL count and focused both sales and marketing on the same revenue and pipeline metrics. In doing so, they eliminated all debate about who (sales or marketing) originated a lead, because in an account-based model the distinction is irrelevant. Instead, the marketing metrics focus on which campaigns are driving engagement within target accounts, throughout their entire path to purchase. It also focused heavily on ROI and the pipeline-to-spend ratio, to ensure that marketing dollars were driving pipeline and a solid return on investment.

The results

The results were remarkable. Three key elements were measured.

○ First and foremost, revenue contribution; 80% of all enterprise revenue was generated through the ABM program efforts.

○ 3X improvement in opportunity-creation rates for those accounts that were part of the ABM program versus those accounts that were generated through other means. This signals that the right accounts were being targeted and the marketing campaigns were more effective.

○ Display ads served to ABM program accounts increased conversion rates of direct mail, email and other channel programs from 50% to 200%.

[SOURCE: Special thanks to Julia Stead, Director of Demand Generation at Invoca for sharing her story and to Terminus for making the introduction.]

HOW TO SET UP YOUR ACCOUNT BASED MARKETING PROGRAM

There are five steps to creating an Account Based Marketing program that converts.

1. **Define goals** — Identify ABM-related business KPIs that will be shared by the sales and marketing team. This will include revenue and pipeline metrics, but may also include strategic goals such as segment penetration, awareness within your targeted accounts (measured by email opt-ins, open rates and inbound inquires) and the number of references secured that match your ideal customer profile.

2. **Select accounts** — Align the team around a list of target accounts that are most likely to deliver against agreed-upon KPIs. This selection and scoring process needs to go beyond simple segmentation like company size and industry. You need to consider intelligence you have on accounts—or add intelligence from third-party vendors. Consider what competitors they have, what is happening in the context of their business, what previous interactions with your business you can learn from, their installed technology stacks, and more.

   While much of this work can be completed by marketing, it's important that you build in time for manual sales team reviews. Selecting accounts must be a collaborative effort in order for the program to be successful.

3. **Assess and refine contact database** — Identify all members of the buying committee who trigger, champion and influence the purchase process at each of your target accounts. Once you have identified all the contact roles you want to pursue, it's likely you will have significant gaps in your database in both record completeness and coverage across all key roles.

   At this point you'll want to do a comprehensive audit to identify where gaps exist. In the audit include a list of all your target accounts, and a matrix of the roles you want to target. Then map this against your database to find out what is missing. If you are serving multiple geographies, be sure to take this into account during your audit.

   When evaluating the database, make sure you not only have email and phone information, but also physical mailing addresses. When targeting key executives, high-impact direct mail can be an effective part of an ABM program.

Sample Matrix:

The example below outlines a fairly simple buying committee for accounting software at a small professional services firm.

Account Name	Owner/ President			CFO			Controller		
	Mailing Address	Phone	Email	Mailing Address	Phone	Email	Mailing Address	Phone	Email
ABC, Inc	X	X		X	X				
Big Money, LLC							X	X	X
...									

If you have a data-savvy operations team member on staff or a small target account list, you can complete a gap analysis internally, but otherwise you'll want to work with a third party to ensure data quality. You need a reference database to compare your data against to determine whether phone numbers are accurate, mailing addresses are valid, contacts still work at the organization, and whether email addresses are deliverable.

Where gaps exist in data integrity or completeness—and there will be some—build a contact development plan. Be careful not to acquire data for roles that do not influence your purchase decisions.

There are four approaches you can leverage to fill gaps.

1. Use a data append service to fill in missing information and correct bad data.

2. Run database building programs. These are not designed to generate leads, but to collect contact information. Surveys, content syndication and sponsored events are often useful in this effort, although costs can add up quickly with this method.

3. Subscribe to data services and purchase data from reputable services. This is effective for many roles in the prospects organization, but is less accurate when the roles you target are highly specialized.

4. Leverage your sales team to complete data.

Most organizations will use a combination of methods to maximize data accuracy and coverage.

Mini Case Study: Not All Data Is Good Data

With thousands of customers, this software company grew their contact database substantially over the years. In fact, they had over 213,000 records, but they learned that data is only as valuable as it is accurate.

Under pressure to improve conversion rates and stimulate additional growth, the organization looked closely at ways to optimize targeting and validate data quality. A health check was conducted that routed contacts through a series of hygiene treatments, including email verification and social screening. This process uncovered significant quality concerns. Email verification not only isolated undeliverable emails, but also found 675 high-risk contacts (i.e., likely spam traps). More strategically, a social screen identified additional problematic contacts representing 13.1% of the database. These contacts passed email verification but social intelligence signaled they were no longer employed at the company indicated on the record.

Upon completion of the health check, a contact gap analysis was helpful in two ways. First, it pinpointed approximately 1,000 accounts whereby neither the client nor the data vendor could identify a single contact. These accounts were sidelined and manually reviewed. Over 80% of them were deemed invalid (i.e., out of business, duplicate company, or found to be a subsidiary). Second, the gap results showed that just under 40% of all contacts met target profile conditions.

Armed with the gap results, the data vendor designed a contact acquisition strategy to identify the most strategic contacts across the named accounts. These contacts were sourced, cleansed, enriched and delivered to the marketing operations group for persona mapping and import.

The numbers added up to offer a significantly improved database, forming a solid foundation for future sales and marketing efforts. For this company the health check and contact discovery efforts led to the following:

○ 30,000 updated job titles

○ 44,643 bad contacts removed

○ 24% of accounts removed from targeting based on erroneous information

○ 45% of the data able to be socially verified as accurate

○ 12,600 new contacts added

[**SOURCE:** Example courtesy of Brian Hession at Oceanos]

4. **Align content strategy and editorial calendar** to ensure that you have appropriate messaging prepared for each member of the buying committee. You'll want to leverage existing content, but seek opportunities to augment these assets with account-specific messages.

5. **Nurture relationships** Develop a steady cadence of sales *and* marketing interactions targeting all relevant buyers within targeted accounts. These interactions can be activated based on agreed-upon triggers that will prompt both sales and marketing actions.

Sample triggers:

Sales adds a new contact to the database	Marketing triggers an email campaign that promotes assets that others in the account have previously downloaded.
A proposal is sent to the champion at the account	Marketing triggers an email to the champion with a business case creation tool, while an email to the economic buyer is triggered with ROI case study content.
A demonstration has been completed	Marketing triggers a survey to demonstration participants at the account collecting feedback on what they observed.
Three different people download content from the website within 30 days	Marketing assigns a follow-up task to the account manager in sales to follow up and qualify the opportunity.
A lead at a targeted account downloads an RFP template	Marketing sends case studies to other buying contacts at the account and triggers a task for sales to follow up.
A contact at a targeted account registers for an event	Marketing assigns a follow-up task to sales for them to invite other contacts at the account to the event that their peer registered to attend.
The account champion completes a self-assessment tool	The results of the self-assessment are shared with other contacts at the account via a marketing triggered email.

If your organization is starting on the journey to Account Based Marketing, or if you've been executing a partial strategy for some time, I hope this has given you fresh ideas to get on track. Remember, no effective marketing tactic is one-size-fits-all, and the same applies to account-based strategies.

CHAPTER 7

Outbound Calling: The Tactic We Love to Hate

If you ever want to make a group of marketers uncomfortable, ask them if their sales team makes cold calls. Watch as everyone's eyes shift downward and they look uncomfortable, until one bold marketer claims, "Of course not, we are 100% inbound marketing," at which point everyone else at the table shrugs and looks ashamed.

The truth is, that one bold marketer who said "of course not" was either lying or in some serious denial. If you walk by your sales team and it's quiet, start to worry.

In a complex B2B sale, your sales team should be actively helping buyers make decisions, not simply taking orders. People who take orders are called customer service, not sales.

The popularity of the term *inbound marketing* by vendors of that technology has made so-called *outbound calling* an almost taboo practice. But the truth is, everybody does it, even the aforementioned vendors. The majority of companies that are growing a business in the world of B2B employ the use of outbound calling tactics.

Outbound outreach isn't the sweatshop atmosphere of dozens of people crammed on the phone calling strangers who want nothing more than to hang up on them. Outbound calling happens every day in very average ways:

○ Does your sales team follow up on web leads?

○ How often does your sales team call a contact that had previous interest but never moved forward?

- Is your sales team reaching out via LinkedIn to schedule introductory calls?

- Does your sales team reach out to decision makers they haven't yet met to validate the purchasing process at a prospect account?

- Have your field sales representatives ever called a prospect to set up an in-person meeting?

If you answered yes to any of these questions, congratulations—you are leveraging "outbound calling." Every effective sales team does it, and they should, because it works.

- Your sales team has a 56% greater chance to attain quota if you engage buyers before they contact a seller[15]

- Forrester Research shows the odds of winning the sale are 74% when you reach decision makers in time to help set their buying vision.[16]

I believe one of the most common reasons marketers are uncomfortable talking about outbound calling is a relatively simple one. Here's the truth: most organizations execute outbound calling poorly. Many inside sales teams are measured by dials, talk times and connects. While these are certainly *indicators* of activity, measuring activity such as this incentivizes the wrong behaviors. It creates artificial pressure to "feed the engine" and game the system, causing ineffective practices to become commonplace. In my practice I've seen five major offenses that reside in the realm of outbound calling.

Offense #1—The Lazy Lunkhead

This is by far the most common offense. When was the last time you heard this one: "Hi, my name is Jack, and I'm calling from XYZ company. I'd like to schedule 15 minutes to learn about your marketing plans." It's easy to visualize Jack sitting at his desk with his feet propped up. Jack has given the person he called absolutely no reason to take time out of their busy day (even 15 minutes) to tell him about their

---

15 https://business.linkedin.com/content/dam/business/sales-solutions/global/en_US/c/pdfs/linkedin-sbi-sales-research-report-us-en-130920.pdf

16 http://blogs.forrester.com/mark_lindwall/14-01-27-to_win_against_increasing_competition_equip_your_salespeople_with_a_deeper_understanding_of_your_buy

plans. It would have taken approximately 2 minutes for him to do a web search on the company he is calling, where he'd learn a lot about their primary business, value propositions and recent accomplishments. Then, maybe he could have crafted a related story about how he can improve what they are doing, or save them money—or maybe even just sounded as though he cared that his prospect's time was valuable.

Offense #2—The Know-It-All

These offenders have made it past the initial hurdle and said something that caught a prospect's attention. Now they start to talk specifics about the prospect's business model. But wait! The offender tells the prospect that their business model is broken because it doesn't fit how their company does business. Word to the wise: unless you sell services to optimize business models, *don't* waste your time trying to fix them. Listen carefully, then do the legwork to figure out how you *can* meet their needs.

Offense #3—The Fraternity/Sorority Recruiter

"I'm reaching out to you because everyone has been telling me about your company"— this is one of those faux promises that buyers sniff out right away. Some callers may consider this a clever way to get a prospect's attention, but it's entirely sneaky and untrue. It only sets both parties up for disappointment. Do you have real case studies from which they can learn? Did a particular person within the company identify them as needing your product or service? If so, use them; if not, skip the clever tricks because they don't build relationships.

Offense #4—The Clinger

Nine out of 10 times when I answer the phone to an unsolicited caller, it is by mistake. I didn't check caller ID, I thought it was someone else or momentarily let my guard down during Thursday sangria afternoon celebrations. So when a salesperson asks if I have time to chat, and I say no, I mean it. (Hint: so do the rest of the people they are calling.) Sellers should take the time to ask their prospect one important question that can be answered in 10 seconds, then ask to send them some follow-up materials instead of torturing both of them with a painful and unwanted conversation.

Offense #5—The Scatterbrain

Have you ever received a call from someone you spoke to last week and they act as if you've never spoken before? The scatterbrain doesn't prepare for calls or even look at past CRM history notes. (There likely aren't any for them to reference, because they forget to take notes). Every dial is like an adventure into the unknown.

With these poor approaches it takes dozens of calls to make a single connection; most calls end with no next step and what we learn during calls ends up in notebooks, not databases. There are some tried and true methods for addressing these common offenses.

Don't give in to the stereotypes.

There are some excellent, helpful inside salespeople out there—I know, because I've done business with them. For those who haven't quite mastered the art, marketing can help by playing an active role in both their development and their ongoing success.

Get beyond training—start coaching.

As marketers we train the sales team on campaigns, promotions and our products and services. We even go as far as to train the team on buyer preferences. But when it comes to the softer, personal-relations skills necessary for outbound calling, we leave training to the sales manager. Not being present to guide the softer skills is a huge missed opportunity to support the sales manager in achieving their goals.

One way to help is to routinely listen to calls. Whether you sit side by side with the sales team, or replay recordings, you will not only find ways to help improve call scripts, you'll learn what's resonating, and what's not, with your targeted buyers to inform new sales tools and offers.

Don't be afraid to jump in and offer advice, especially if you can point callers toward a particular asset or series of qualification questions they hadn't considered using.

Schedule a call blitz.

A call blitz is a focused full day of calling on prospects or customers as part of a sales program. It has a specific offer, targeted list and short-term goal(s). It is often accompanied by additional incentives for callers and a rally atmosphere from sales management. It differs from any other day in a call center/sales office by its intensity and focus. At the end of this chapter you will see a bonus how-to section on how to run an effective call blitz.

Help sales give.

The most effective outbound calling teams build relationships with their buyers by always being ready to give in return for information they want to collect. Marketing plays an important role in developing valuable content, insights and assets that sales can share on the phone and in personalized email communications. I don't mean product-related materials; I mean leveraging your sales team as a distribution channel for your thought leadership content, third-party licensed content, or other marketing assets meant to inform or educate your prospects.

Make it an expectation to capture sales phone activity.

Using conversations to trigger marketing is the inverse of what most of us do, but it can be a valuable collaboration technique. In Chapter 9, Catching Turtles, we will discuss how to nurture prospects. This is incredibly important for generating interest. Unfortunately, most nurturing programs are blind to and disconnected from the phone conversations sales is using to engage the same prospects. It doesn't have to be this way. With disciplined use of a CRM system, it is possible to prompt communications based on sales interactions with buyers.

For example, you might experiment with some of these simple triggers that can all be sent automatically when actions are taken within your CRM system:

- Voicemail left — What happens after a voicemail is left by your sales team? My guess is it varies from one rep to the next. Some follow up with email, some reach out via LinkedIn, some simply schedule another callback. Wouldn't it be great to add some consistency by automatically triggering email communication that matched the stage of the opportunity?

- Sales proposal sent — When a sales proposal is sent, you know the deal is maturing. This is a good time to implement a case study nurture stream.

- New competitor added to the opportunity — When the salesperson adds a new competitor to an opportunity within the CRM, marketing has learned something very important about which solutions the buyer is considering. By developing content assets that specifically address your advantages over that competitor, you can trigger automatic communications that complement the effort of your calling team.

- ○ Post demo/meeting survey — when the initial demo/meeting is completed, consider sending out a link to a simple survey. Keep it short, with no more than four questions.

SAMPLE:

Thank you for taking time out of your busy schedule to attend a demonstration of Acme's time-saving technology. How'd we do?

How relevant was the demonstration you attended to your day-to-day responsibilities?
1 – Not relevant at all
2 – Somewhat relevant
3 – Totally relevant

Did the demonstration influence your interest in purchasing Acme products?
1 – Less likely to purchase
2 – No impact on purchase intent
3 – More likely to purchase

What was the most compelling capability we showed?

What do you wish you had seen but didn't?

We covered a lot of material during the demo, so if you have any follow-up questions please don't hesitate to reach out.

CASE STUDY: SAY GOODBYE TO NO-SHOWS

Never underestimate the power of follow-through on calling efforts.

The Challenge

I had been working for the past few months to ready a client's sales team for their new product introduction. They did everything right: lots of up-front research, tons of testing with real users and good old-fashioned hard work. It was time to bring the product to market. The value proposition was working, and their target buyers were accepting discovery and demo meetings, when suddenly their momentum hit a wall. The sales team would dial in to scheduled meetings only to find deafening silence 30–40% of the time. The no-shows were consistent across several different sales people.

Of course the sales team would reach back out to the absentees. They received a lot of apologies and agreement to reschedule. It was clear the value proposition was compelling, but something happened in the time between the meeting confirmation and when the demo was to be held. Were we doing a good job of making the calendar invite as compelling as our conversation had been? The clear answer was no.

As happens with many professionals, once the meeting was secured, little attention was put on the calendar invite details or subject line. Our missed opportunity was right there in the details of the calendar invite.

It's a long road from verbally accepting a meeting to actually showing up. Our buyers are very busy. Their day is filled with all kinds of commitments. Once they got off the phone with us, the excitement of our conversation faded into another input to remember, and the appointment was just another block on a busy day.

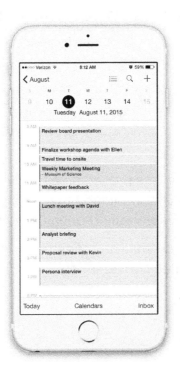

With the way we had been sending calendar invitations, our best argument for why the prospect should show up was either not present at all in the appointment, or hidden in the meeting notes that don't show up on a typical calendar scan.

The Solution

We made three important recommendations:

1. We challenged ourselves to create subject lines that addressed these two questions:

    A. When our guest scans their calendar to accommodate an unexpected need, does our invite stand out as important?

    B. Have we done a good job of reminding our audience why they agreed to the meeting in the first place?

    I challenge you to do the same. Below you'll see sample calendar subject lines transformed into value propositions to get your creative juices flowing. The goal is to be descriptive, but also to reinforce the larger story you want to tell.

Avoid these...	Try something like this...
Demo	3x More Effective Content Demo
Follow Up	Market Research Interview Confirmed
Acme Corp Meeting	Finalize Contract Terms
Interview	Sept 3rd Workshop Agenda Review
Proposal	ROI Analysis Results for Cable Corp

2. We ensured that everyone was presetting a meeting alert to notify attendees either 5 or 15 minutes before the scheduled time. This is standard functionality in most email systems, but not everyone had been using it.

3. We worked hard to ensure that as many meetings as possible were scheduled within 48 hours of the initial conversation.

The Results

By implementing these simple changes, no-show rates dropped from over 30% to only 10%.

As professionals, we work really hard to establish a rapport with a prospective buyer. In some cases we've spent weeks or months nurturing our relationship. It's time we spent as much time considering the meeting subject line as we would the email subject line of our outbound communications. Those few extra seconds can go a long way toward improving not only meeting attendance, but the quality of the conversation itself.

HOW-TO GUIDELINES: RUN A BLITZ LIKE THE PROS

Leveraging a call blitz is a fantastic way to shake up the routine of your sales team and begin a more collaborative approach to outbound calling. Because of its full-day focus and highly specific offer and targets, it's an infusion of energy and motivation.

Why plan a call blitz?

There is a lot of science to selling, but there is just as much emotion. Call blitz campaigns are about stirring up emotion, taking an ordinary week and making it extraordinary. It should be viewed as a momentum trigger, not a sustainable revenue engine.

The six-ingredient recipe for a foolproof call blitz

1. Instant gratification — Salespeople are humans (contrary to most caricatures of them) and like all people they are motivated by competition. In order to create intensity, you need to create incentives that are tangible and achievable on the same day. For complex products, consider rewarding the team for new relevant names added to the database, client referrals secured, demonstrations booked, or quotes distributed. Make sure your prizes are visually displayed in front of the team, and create multiple ways to win throughout the day. If you only have one or two "master" prizes, energy will ebb and flow. Set prizes for first, most, best and team goals that scale in value accordingly. Don't forget—money is always appreciated, but not a good call blitz incentive. Instead, give out tickets to a big game, or look for unusual experiences like a luxury car rental or gift certificate to a hot restaurant. Good salespeople can buy what they want, but they love the thrill of a contest. Kick off with a bang in the morning, and reenergize post-lunch with a surprise contest or two.

2. Compelling offer — It's not enough for your sales team to have a good reason (those prizes) for achieving above-normal goals. You must arm them with an offer that prospects will find compelling. You can consider offers such as:

- Special pricing — Price promotions can often provide an incentive to move forward sooner than originally planned. But only when the prospect already has an interest in your product *and* they believe the pricing being offered is truly a limited-time offer. Make sure promotional pricing has a clear end date and is compelling enough to spur action. Keep in mind that special pricing does not always have to be a discount. It can be an extra bonus that is given upon purchase—for example, tickets to a popular industry conference, or free training.

- New product introductions — When you are introducing a new product to market call blitz campaigns can be very effective. Build a "breaking news" or "exclusive preview" program that gives your audience the feeling of getting something special. New product introductions are also great for going back to happy customers with another way you can serve their needs and build on the rapport you have already established.

- Event registration — Driving attendance at upcoming events can also be a compelling platform for a call blitz. Be sure to reward registrations, but also set an expectation that attendance is important. Events that are educational in nature vs. product oriented work most effectively.

3. The right list — You can build the most effective offer and put great prizes in front of sales and still fail. Call blitz campaigns only work when you have a targeted, warm list of prospects to call. The list you pull will be specific to the offer the team is promoting. Some examples include:

Limited-Time Pricing	<ul><li>Find prospects who already have familiarity with your product/service. For example, anyone who has had a qualification meeting or demonstration in the last 90 days.</li><li>You may also want to include anyone who had been in your pipeline within the last year but their opportunity was closed due to the prospect not moving forward with any solution.</li><li>Don't forget to include anyone in your active pipeline you are hoping to close in the next 2–4 months. A special pricing promotion might give them urgency to buy now.</li></ul>

New Product Introduction	When introducing a new product, be sure to pull contacts who are likely to benefit from its capabilities.
	○ Seek prospects who have recently engaged with the sales team. For example, having a conversation within the last 90 days. ○ Consider prospects who recently download content about the new product being introduced. Be sure not to include just any content download, but those that were specific to the new product introduction. ○ Include customers for whom this new product will enhance the current product they have purchased, not feel like an overlap of capabilities. ○ Exclude customers who have outstanding support issues or are known to be dissatisfied with their current purchase.
Upgrade Bonus	Sometimes calling on existing customers and promoting an upgrade to a new version of the product they use is an excellent basis for a call blitz. Be sure the sales team will be compensated on these upgrades if you decide to go down this path. When pulling the customer list be sure to exclude anyone who has outstanding support issues or is known to be dissatisfied. The last thing you want is to bring down the team with negative customer feedback.
Event Invitation	Call blitz campaigns are a great way drive event attendance. When pulling the list be sure to consider the following:
	○ The time zone of the attendee for online events. Will the scheduled session be during reasonable working hours? ○ The physical location of those you are calling for in-person events. Is the person likely to be within a reasonable travel distance to the event? ○ Is the event agenda aligned to the interest of the people you are calling? Make sure to segment your list to attract those who will find value in the events content.

4. Shake up the environment — A call blitz day should not feel like any other day. Shake up teams, set out lunch and breakfast, bring in an afternoon ice cream bar. Skip the bagels and pizza and focus on high protein/energy foods that are going to boost energy. Visually track performance and make some noise. One of my clients even asked everyone to dress up—Halloween in May, why not? The team costumes were hysterical and a great way not to take ourselves too seriously. When the energy is high in the room, prospects on the other end of the line feel it.

5. Teamwork — Individual incentives drive activity, but you also want to evoke teamwork. Group callers into teams, and recognize both team and individual achievements to keep the spirit of cooperation in full swing. Consider creative team names, and eat breakfast and lunch together.

6. Cheerleader/Executive sponsor — As with any good sports performance, you need a facilitator to keep energy up, congratulate the successes and coax non-performers to play the game. The blitz is most effective if the facilitator is not the sales manager. While sales managers play a role, call blitz efforts work best when the reps feel pressure to perform above normal.

Call blitz campaigns can be incredibly effective, but there are common mistakes you must avoid to optimize their value.

○ There is too much of a good thing — Call blitz campaigns work because of their intensity and focus. They are great ways to kick off momentum around a new theme or offer. It's tempting to want a call blitz to happen every week. Falling for this temptation is one of the biggest mistakes organizations make. While there is no magic number of days required between call blitzes I generally find 8–10-week breaks are optimal.

○ Go big or go home — If you don't have all six ingredients for your call blitz, don't do one. The worst thing you can do is get everybody jazzed for a momentum trigger that results in a lackluster day that feels like any other day. Call blitzes are emotional stimulants, and you must hit all the hot spots to be effective.

○ Avoid setting the wrong goals — Call blitz campaigns work when you set aggressive but achievable goals. If no one believes they can meet the goals, no one will try. Another common mistake is setting long-term goals as a way to measure and reward participants. Without instant gratification, call blitz efforts fall flat.

SECTION 3

BUYER INSIGHTS & MARKETING FUNDAMENTALS

CHAPTER 8

Go-to-Market: Say Goodbye to Ready–Sell–Aim

The claim that 80–95% of product launches fail has been generally dismissed as legend, but a variety of more empirical studies show that 35–40% of B2B product launches fail to hit revenue momentum. No matter which data you believe, the risk of failure is high, due in part to how we plan our go-to-market strategies.

In our effort to get to market quickly, many product launches (for the balance of this chapter "product" refers to services as well as products) fail because they take a ready–sell–aim approach.

Ready — After some minimum set of product capabilities are met and tested, we declare victory and attempt to drive adoption. Although some early market research is conducted, this approach is highly product-centric and decisions such as release schedules revolve around development milestones.

Sell — Anxious to get product feedback, we unleash our product on a sales team. We assume they will figure out who the ideal customer is by trial and error. Until then, we provide a series of generalized assets focused on our product's value proposition, and point sales in the direction we think is most likely to succeed.

Aim — Based on early victories, we aim and calibrate our subsequent sales and marketing efforts to attempt to replicate those first successes.

Not only is this approach common, but our industry also spends a fair amount of effort justifying it as the most effective. We call it agile and lean. While these are all noble attributes, we've applied them haphazardly to product launch, resulting in a ready–sell–aim model, which is flawed.

The truth is, unfocused learning is too slow to prepare us for a successful product launch. Without doing the up-front work to ready our sales efforts, an undisciplined approach to learning is applied at a crucial time when every lesson informs how the business moves forward.

Another common flaw with this model is the fact that ad hoc early successes don't always lead to long-term sustainability. When our sales team is left to find early customers with minimum direction, they default to their friends and familiar network, plus any low-hanging fruit they can find. While this may appear to fuel the engine, it does not always align to long-term market viability.

To avoid these mistakes, we must scale slower to build longevity. In the early days of a product launch everything we do is the foundation for what we do next. When early efforts are ad hoc we have to pause not only to reflect but also to document where we started.

I've spent the better part of two decades launching new products to market and introducing mature products to new audiences. While each effort is unique, there are common considerations that, when implemented, improve your chances of triumph.

Introducing Aim–Ready–Sell

This reorientation is essential for giving your product the best chance of sustainable market viability.

Aim — Instead of orienting around what you are building, structure your go-to-market plans around who you plan to serve. In this model, you iterate product development in direct contact with buyers, and formally test value propositions and product capabilities long before trying to sell the solution. Buyers don't always know what they want, so be sure your market research tests your hypotheses, rather than accepting only what users say they want.

The most common mistake companies make when releasing new products is trying to serve too broad an audience. Don't be afraid to narrow your focus from everyone who could benefit from your offering to a segment you can serve well and ultimately dominate.

Ready — There is no way to anticipate every need prior to a product's launch, but there are some essential requirements you should seek to address before seeking to scale a sales organization around its launch. You should not only focus this information gathering on product maturity, but also message validation and an easily identifiable ideal customer profile. In the early days your product owners (likely a founder, if you're a startup organization, or a product manager in a more mature organization) are also your evangelists and best salespeople. Until you have a proven market and a repeatable process for tackling it, scaling a sales organization is a waste of money and time. A product is not considered "ready" to scale into sales until you have an ideal customer profile that has gone through a fair amount of due diligence.

Sell — Don't misunderstand—selling happens to some extent before you're entirely ready. In fact, we sell our ideas long before they become a product. The most frequently misunderstood decision is when to introduce a formal sales team to a product for launch. In the aim–ready–sell model, a formal sales team is only staffed once a predictable process has been established. For large companies that means experimenting with a subset of your sales power before general adoption across the entire team. Once that process has been identified, you'll want to test it at scale—at which point training a sales team and developing a technology platform to capture future learnings is essential.

All product launches involve iterative learning, but with careful planning you can learn deliberately to accelerate growth or redirect your focus as the market warrants.

HOW-TO GUIDELINES: MANAGE A PRODUCT LAUNCH

Launching a new product can be exhilarating and overwhelming at the same time. While multiple people will be responsible for managing portions of your go-to-market efforts, I've found it essential to assign an overall program manager. The program manager's job is not to execute all the tasks but rather to monitor progress against them and ensure that high-risk items are resourced appropriately. Their most valuable skill set is an ability to communicate and motivate a wide range of personalities.

> The aim–ready–sell launch template can help you stay organized. Download your complimentary copy at (www.unleashpossible.com/templates)

Below I've compiled the most common challenges marketers face when building a launch plan. The following principles apply whether you are launching a new product to market, or introducing a mature product to a new audience.

1. Narrow your ideal customer profile.

This is a very critical step, which will determine who you test messages against, who you train sales to target, who is recruited to test your offering, and how you prioritize product and service requirements. It is probably the hardest decision your team will make because, like many organizations, you may struggle to narrow your focus.

Presumably, before you decided to build a product or design your service offering you had visions of who your offering would help. You've likely spent weeks and months convincing people "the market is huge" so they would invest in your idea. Now that you're leading up to the big launch day, it's time to narrow your audience—considerably. Some products fail because product owners never built what was intended, but most fail because what they intended was not focused enough on a specific audience.

When building your ideal customer profile (ICP) you must take into account not only who will benefit from your solution, but also who else is competing for their mindshare and where your strengths lie across the organization. Remember that your ICP does not comprise all the companies you can ever serve, but those that you can dominate in the initial launch effort. Ask yourself the following questions to prepare your ICP ahead of launch:

What roles within the buyer's organization will benefit most from my offering?

What industries are most likely to exhibit a pain that my solution solves?

- Are any special certifications required to serve these vertical markets?
- Which markets have people on my team already served for which we can tap into their expertise and knowledge?
- Does one industry have a larger number of organizations than the others I could target?
- Is there an industry that the competition is not serving well today?

What size organizations should I target?

- How long a sales cycle am I prepared to resource?
- Does the size of the organization have an impact on the level of pain my solution solves?
- Will smaller organizations have trouble funding my product?
- What payment methods am I prepared to accept?
- Does the number of people in a particular role make a difference?

What geography can I support?

- Where is my staff located?
- How much infrastructure do I have in place to support multiple time zones?
- Where is the buying authority likely to be for the companies I am targeting?

What other attributes signal a readiness for my product?

- Does their technology environment either complement or indicate an upgrade to my product?
- What actions might trigger a need for my offering?
- Does it matter how large a customer base they have?

2. Be brutal about message testing.

Once your ICP is determined, it is time to test not only your offer but also your value propositions. Too often our core messages are defined by one of two largely irrelevant audiences—those that gave us money to fund our effort and the preferences of the executive committee or development team. Neither is a good measure of how your buyers will respond.

I'll never forget learning this lesson firsthand while launching a data warehouse appliance to market at Dataupia.* We were certain the product name would be Dataupia Data Warehouse Appliance. We thought it conveyed easy-to-use, low-maintenance hardware. (I know—not at all sexy, but we felt it was descriptive.) While doing other message testing, we threw in the product name at the last minute. Boy, was I glad we did! It turned out our buyers' hated the word *appliance*. Universally, 100% of the people we spoke with at the time said they did not trust appliances with their data. It was a total turn-off! Although we continued to sell a data warehouse appliance, it was clear that this moniker would not suffice as our product name. As a young company, we didn't need to add trust issues to our new product introduction. We ended up naming the product the Dataupia Satori Server, since *server* was a term our target buyer was much more comfortable trusting. The experience was a testament to our need to get outside perspective and include testing with buyers in our message development efforts.

Once a product is launched, you will refine messages over time via various testing methods including A/B testing, copy & imagery experiments on your website and in your email models, and of course via feedback from the sales team and broader community. However, effective product launches don't go blindly into launch: time is spent up front with qualitative message testing efforts.

Before testing messages the first thing you need to do is document your core value proposition. I find it helpful to test the elements in the chart below, because they make up the foundation of your message framework. When building your testing guide, remember that you should already have built personas and validated high-level value propositions at this stage (see Chapter 10 to learn how). In this process, you are now working to refine the words and phrases you use to describe your value proposition.

Message Element	Descriptor	Testing Method
Product Name	Don't expect to find a single product name as a clear "winner," but you can identify product names that turn off your audience and should be avoided.	Provide participants a list of 5–7 product names and ask them to rank their top three choices and to cross out any names that turn them off. I like to do this after participants have seen a description of the product offering for context. Once completed, ask them to explain why certain names turned them off, and what it was about the first choice that attracted them.
100-Word Product Description	I recommend putting together three 100-word product descriptors to compare.	Ask participants to read one at a time. After each one, ask them to rate on a scale of 1 to 5 how compelled they would be to learn more based only on the description. (1–not at all, 5–very much.) It's best to test these messages with at least some people who have not seen a demo or are not very familiar with your offering. Then ask them to cross out words that turn them off, highlight those that compel them and underline anything they find confusing.

Message Element	Descriptor	Testing Method
Capability Statements	Capability statements should be bullets or short sentences that describe what your offering does/includes. I like to test 6–8 statements with the goal of finding the top 3 most compelling per persona.	Ask participants, on a scal[...] of an impact each stateme[...] work. (1–no impact, 5–very impactful.)
Benefit Statements	Benefit statements should be bullets or short sentences that describe how your offering benefits users. I like to test 6–8 statements with the goal of finding the top 3 most compelling statement per persona.	Ask participants, on a scale of 1 to 5, how much of an impact each statement would have on their work. (1–no impact, 5–very impactful.) Then ask them to rate on the same scale how credible each statement is coming from a vendor. (1–not trustworthy, 5–very trustworthy.) Your objective is to find the intersection of high-impact benefits and credible statements.
2–4 Differentiators	Differentiators must be unique to you, easy to prove and important to the buyer.	Ask participants to indicate whether each differentiator is unique in the market, using a true-or-false response. Then ask participants to rate on a scale of 1 to 5 how important it is to their job. (1–not at all important, 5–very important.)
1-Minute Elevator Pitch Persona A	Your elevator pitch should be no more than 2–4 sentences in length and designed to be spoken, not read. So feel free to be more conversational in your tone than you might be in the other sections.	Ask participants to read the pitch and rate on a scale of 1 to 5 how compelled they would be to learn more based only on the statement. (1–not at all, 5–very much.) Then, ask them to cross out words that turn them off, highlight those that compel them and underline anything they find confusing.
1-Minute Elevator Pitch Persona B		
1-Minute Elevator Pitch Persona C		

Be sure to test your messages across all critical personas on the buying committee, not just the users of your offering.

* Thank you to Elaine Salloway of Salloway & Associates Research for bringing us the right audience and thoroughly testing our assumptions.

5. Price for adoption.

Pricing has a huge impact on both the speed of market adoption and also the long-term viability of an offering. It's incredibly important to take several factors into account when determining price.

First, document the actual cost of your offering — both the cost to serve and the anticipated cost to sell. Even if profitability is not your priority at launch, you need to understand the implications on your business. You might be surprised to learn, for example, that it costs as much to serve your largest client as your smallest.

Next, consider what others are charging. Be sure to include not only direct competitors, but also the price of alternative approaches to solving the problem you address.

Last, test different pricing models with your target buyers. When it comes to pricing, customers can rarely provide an accurate assessment of exact price. To get at the facts you need, ask probing questions, such as:

- What percentage of your budget is allocated toward solving _____? (Describe the pain you solve.)

- What is your buying authority in dollars before you have to seek approvals from a budgeting committee or other authority?

- How has the budget for X changed from last year? (Decreased, increased, remained the same.)

- What would you expect to pay for a product that could do X? (Note: Go ahead and ask, but be careful not to interpret the answer literally. Buyers never tell the truth here.)

- How much does X pain impact your organization in dollars per year?

- If you were to purchase a product that could do X, how would you prefer to pay?
    - Monthly fee
    - Annual fee
    - One-time fee
    - Other — please explain

- If you were to purchase a product that could do X, what additional fees would you expect to accompany a license cost?

Freemium models

One common mistake marketers make is to assume that in order to drive adoption they must have a free version of the offering, often referred to as a "freemium model." While there are examples of massive market dominance based on free, most don't survive. I advise my clients to ask this critical question when considering giving away their product or service: "How much change is required by the organization to use my service?"

If an individual can act alone and gain value without involving others, freemium might be worth considering as a seeding strategy. If you decide to go that route, be sure you have a clear path to making money—either through upgrading capabilities or selling complimentary services to free users.

But if processes must be changed or multiple people in an organization need to adapt the way they work to see the benefit of your solution, freemium is perhaps not the best approach. I've found that paying for something shows a level of commitment that accessing a free service does not indicate, and that organizational change requires commitment by your champion.

A software company that sold a content marketing service recently struggled with this very issue. After extensive research they launched an early version of their product aimed at senior content marketers who were looking to scale their efforts. Within 60 days of launch they had 10 paying customers at, or close to, the list price they had set ($1,000/month). Anxious to build on this success. the team hired four full-time salespeople and set very high new customer acquisition goals. Since customer adoption was the primary task at hand, salespeople were paid largely to bring new customers on board, as opposed to drive revenue. The product team wanted to get more people using the system to help set a strong roadmap for future development, while the management team wanted to show exceptional growth to attract investment dollars. In an attempt to do both, they eliminated all fees and gave the product away. With some clever marketing they were able to secure more than 300 subscribers to the service in less than 45 days. Sounds like a happy ending, doesn't it? It wasn't. Of all the free subscribers, fewer than five used the product at all and only two adopted it with regularity. Ironically, those two had been evaluating the product when it was fee-based. Instead of driving product use and showing growth to investors, the company now had significantly lowered its adoption rate and had no proof of a recurring revenue model. They were not able to secure the additional funds they needed to keep growing and had to reduce staff significantly. It's an important lesson that reminds us that the more we ask people to change, the more commitment we need from them in the process.

While pricing will change over time, the sooner you can stabilize a strategy, the easier it will be for your sales team to gain momentum from one quarter to the next.

Once you are armed with data—cost, competition and buyer insights—you can map out a variety of scenarios for the team to consider and project when profitability will be met among estimated levels of adoption. Be sure to take into account how quickly you can not only get buyers interested, but get them using your offering.

4. Secure early advocates.

It's likely that you have a couple of people in your organization who are passionate about your initiative and excellent spokespersons for your new offer. However, to be successful, you'll need more than just internal advocates—you need to secure third parties who validate your message.

You'll want to consider the following groups:

- ❍ Partners — What complementary products or service providers help support your story and can add credibility to your launch?

- ❍ Analysts — Which analysts conduct research into your buying community?

- ❍ Industry influencers — Who is thought of as a leader in your buyer community? Consider bloggers, keynote speakers, authors and anyone with a significant and relevant following. Be sure not to focus solely on the size of their audience. The depth of their influence is critical even if it is among a smaller following.

- ❍ Early adopters — Consider enrolling companies in your early adopter program that not only can provide product feedback, but would make good spokespersons for your value proposition.

Once early advocates are identified, assign a specific program owner to own the relationship and build a game plan for how each will be engaged. It's important to be specific with your intended goal for each relationship.

— 104 —

Sample influencer goal matrix:

Advocate	Relationship Owner	Objective
John Smith, analyst at Hero Worship Firm	Jane in analyst relations	Quote for press release
Samantha Stone, beta tester	Bob – early adopter program manager	Guest blog post, quote for data sheet
Nick Plant, technology partner	Melissa – partner program manager	Partnership press release
David Table, author	Cat – product marketing	Thought leadership whitepaper
…		

While you should never pay for testimonial quotes, making introductions to a peer or references to the press or other customers; some support activities should be budgeted against. Be prepared to pay for third-party support that is time consuming or core to the advocate's business—for example, writing a whitepaper, speaking at a launch event or providing detailed messaging feedback.

CASE STUDY: ZERO TO HERO

There I was, seven months pregnant, and finally resting my swollen feet in my hotel room. I took a deep breath of satisfaction. The last briefing was finished and I would soon be on a plane home.

Sitting next to me was a buzzing server, black, sleek and top secret, the result of many months of market research and engineering mastery. Although the company I worked for had a booth at the trade show put on annually by TDWI (The Data Warehouse Institute), the product we were building had not yet been released. A few weeks before the conference, we had reached out to several industry analysts and speakers and asked them to take a briefing. Our message was all very cloak-and-dagger, asking them to sign a nondisclosure agreement (NDA) before we could show them what we had built. In hindsight I think the NDA helped us secure the meetings because it created an air of mystery at an event that hadn't spurred much dramatic innovation in some time.

During the briefings, we did a small demonstration of our technology, but what really cemented our relationships was our focus on reviewing the market landscape and articulating what we hoped to disrupt. We were up against some very entrenched technology companies and bold in our assertions. But we were smart, and very specific about the types of queries our processor would improve. We knew that our system could support all kinds of analysis, but we also understood that no one would believe sweeping statements from a product owner that did not yet have any paying customers. We had done benchmark testing to prove our claims and we stayed focused on the area where we could add the most value.

It was during this event that we had started our journey to building advocates who would be critical in the early days of selling the solution. The endorsement of these contacts, along with two other groups, was essential for securing us press coverage during our official product release announcement, but more critically it gave us the credibility we needed to solicit CIO meetings at large enterprise organizations where our solution was most valuable. Later we would pay some of these market gurus to write thought leadership papers that discussed issues critical to our audience and validated not only the problem we addressed, but our approach to solving it.

In parallel to soliciting these industry gurus, we also were building partner evangelists. We knew specific applications within telecommunication companies were an excellent fit for us, not only because we could run the analysis very quickly, but equally because our competition had a difficult time with this class of analysis. We also recognized that senior IT professionals at these companies did not know who we were and were averse to risk. With that background, we built a partnership with a revenue assurance application provider that would not only supply some of our first early adopters, but also another critical third-party endorsement for the problem we were addressing.

The last group of advocates came in the form of early adopters themselves. We found a handful of customers who let us test our technology directly against the competition they already had in place. And although we couldn't always use their name, we were able to present the results with enough detail to be trustworthy.

A couple of months later my youngest son was born, and so too was our product. With newborn snuggled in my arms I reviewed the launch press release and wrote the last of the website copy and product collateral. The launch was infinitely more effective because we had spent the prior six months building advocates to help tell our story.

The result:

- ○ Press coverage in every major trade publication we targeted
- ○ Two pages of third-party endorsements
- ○ Most critically: our first paying customers

Perhaps nowhere else in marketing is the saying "Failing to plan is planning to fail" more appropriate than in designing go-to-market strategies. With proper foresight and the investment of time, organizations can achieve proper footing for a successful launch.

CHAPTER 9

Catching Turtles

It's not hard to catch a turtle. They typically lurk in the high grass by the shore, especially near the pond we visit when staying at our house in the mountains. A few years ago my son Johnny and his friends were playing on the beach. Ever the animal lover, he wanted to play with a turtle.

Fully equipped with a net, Johnny was plenty fast in comparison to the lumbering turtle. All he had to do was whisk the net in front of the slow-moving turtle and—voilà—it's caught. But a turtle that's been swooped into a net does not want to be played with. It becomes defensive, retreating into its shell. This turtle curled up and waited to be left alone. He didn't listen to anyone's voice, and it was clear he certainly wasn't going to play with Johnny.

My son was determined to forgo this net business and persuade the turtle to come to him. He asked me to drive him back up to our cottage to get supplies, while instructing his friends to keep the turtle at bay on the beach until he returned. I decided that my trashy summer novel would need to wait while my son embarked on an impromptu science experiment. Little did I know, this was a marketing lesson in the making.

In the house Johnny gathered lettuce, carrots, cheese, chips and a couple of hot dogs. I wondered silently if he was planning a tailgate party instead of catching a turtle, but, eager to get my feet firmly planted back in the sand, I acquiesced. Back on the beach, Johnny strategically placed bits of each type of food acquired in the pantry raid and stepped away. Like a field scientist, he made careful observation of what the turtle was attracted to. The findings? Lettuce and hot dogs earned the most attention from this shy little turtle.

Johnny removed the chips, cheese, and the remainder of the unsuccessful menu and laid out a trail of the turtle's favorite food. Then he sat on the beach a few feet away and waited.

And waited.

And waited some more.

After what felt like an eternity (it turns out turtles are not the fastest creatures), I looked up to see the turtle sitting in front of Johnny, not curled into his shell but confidently taking a small bit of hot dog out of my son's outstretched hand. Johnny is grinning from ear to ear, and I'm standing there with pride—and a slight concern for what's left in the kitchen for lunch.

But then it hit me. My patient son just executed a fantastic marketing campaign. Think about it. Interrupting our buyers is easy—we incessantly email every contact to come into our business. We call out to conference attendees as they walk by our trade show booth. (The name tags make it so easy!) We cold-call office phones which buyers absent-mindedly pick up between meetings. We place a billboard in front of consumers as they drive their daily commute.

There are hundreds of proven tactics for interrupting a buyer, but getting their attention by bothering them has limited value. More often than not, our prospects react like this gentle turtle, by receding into their shell. As we compete for the attention of our overwhelmed prospects, our goal is *not* to bother, but to entice. Johnny figured out how to lure the turtle to him and earn its trust, and that's exactly what marketers must achieve.

We must strive to:

- Provide value, not trick buyers into accidently bumping into our materials
- Take time to understand our buyers deeply before acting rashly
- Consider exactly what action or lesson we want buyers to take from each piece of content we produce
- Trust ourselves enough to have patience to truly learn

CASE STUDY: REDUCING THE AVERAGE SALES CYCLE BY 54 DAYS WITH CUSTOMER-CENTRIC MESSAGING

Does the turtle theory hold up to real marketing goals? Let's explore an example in action.

The Challenge

A B2B technology company in the team collaboration space had just hired me to complete an audit of their lead generation efforts. Their sales cycles were unpredictable, ranging from 30 days to years, and their revenue growth had stagnated.

The Situation

They were strong CRM users, so the database was rich with information. Their prospective customer database was comprehensive and they knew how to articulate their product value proposition. Yet the sales/buying cycle was highly variable and difficult to predict. The company had a robust outbound sales effort, so there was no lack of contact with prospective buyers. Marketing promoted regular web seminars, and sales staff pushed for product demonstrations. Both were effective tools, but something was missing.

The Research

I needed to figure out what was going on. The first step I took was to analyze past program performance, review the quality of the database, interview current customers, and listen in on several prospect calls. What I learned was that the organization was primarily sending product-centric marketing content, followed up by salespeople asking prospects to take a demo. After spending some time with their sales and marketing teams, I found that this company's internal culture was high energy and a little aggressive. Their buyers, on the other hand, were analytical, behind-the-scenes technologists; not exactly a natural match.

And it showed. Historically, every prospect received content centered squarely on the product and its features and benefits. This company approached lead generation with the same tenet of catching a turtle with a net. Inside sales reps would dial 400–800 contacts a week hoping to find a sales-ready lead. When I sat in the sales bullpen I could hear a constant buzz of activity—and a whole lot of hang-ups. By sheer volume, this outreach caught some turtles, but generally they were confused, grumpy and often wanted nothing more than to get off the phone. Of course, that interrupt-driven approach had limits and despite previous growth, the business had hit a plateau.

The Solution

The marketing program we designed would be the organization's first attempt at nurturing prospects with content that was not product-centric, but rather spoke to the issues faced by these technologists. Although the concepts were welcomed, they were foreign. To keep things simple, we divided the database into two segments—those who had already seen a product demo and those who had not. We created a 9-touch email campaign with a consistent theme and visual treatment, but unique offers that spoke directly to the problems faced by our buyers. The emails were distributed about once every other week. We did some basic subject line testing, but nothing more sophisticated than that.

In parallel I also ran sales workshops about the merits of lead nurturing and how to integrate them into their outbound calling efforts. These workshops turned out to be pivotal. (We covered the workshop details in Chapter 3). The first training workshop was run about three weeks before the program went live. The second was done two touches into the program.

The Results

After the first six touches, the campaign had already generated results, shaving 38 days off the sales cycle. The control group that was not included in the new campaigns took, on average, 104 days to move from demo to product evaluation. Those who were nurtured took only 66 days. What's more, those who were nurtured spent only 40 days between evaluating the product and technical selection. Those who were not took 56 days.

Our new approach shaved a total of 54 days off the sales process, adding up to significant bottom-line benefits. With this kind of improvement in efficiency, the company saw greater productivity per sales representative. By reducing the amount of time it took to close a sale by nearly two months, each sales rep was now closing more deals each month than before.

Think about the hard costs associated with this business. Imagine the average sales rep was making about $65,000 annually, and closing three deals a month. If each sale is approximately $10,000, each rep closes 36 deals, or $360,000 annually. By increasing the quality of the leads each rep worked with and improving the speed at which deals are done, a campaign like this could drive more deals than before. In this scenario, if nine more deals closed in the same amount of time, each $65k/year sales rep could now drive $450,000 annually with 45 deals, rather than 36: a 25% increase in revenue.

What made the difference?

- ❍ **Database segmentation** — The company had spent a lot of money building a database of target accounts and contact names, but most campaigns historically were segmented only by geography. For our new program, we created specific messaging tracks based on prior interactions with the sales team.

- ❍ **New messaging** — Before jumping in to create assets, I interviewed a dozen customers. (I cover how to conduct these interviews in Chapter 10.) The resulting insights formed the foundation for new messaging that was centered on the buyer, not the product.

- ❍ **Invested in imagery** — We invested in custom imagery and a unified campaign look and feel that matched the tone and passions of their buyers. We even made posters for the lobby entrance using these images.

- ❍ **Loads of new content** — From interactive calculators to research reports, whitepapers and how-to guides, we invested in a new set of assets that were helpful and educational in nature. To avoid a long program delay, we repurposed existing materials while we built the new materials in parallel.

This case study reminds us that you really can jump right into the nurturing pool by changing your focus from your products to buyer pains and see an almost immediate benefit.

With the best of intentions we're often tempted to map out a complex program that takes ages to implement and will make a huge splash. It's easy to forget that simple programs work, and may often be the best way to get started. After all, you need to see results— fast.

HOW-TO GUIDELINES: LEAD NURTURING

1. Start with a map.

Building a lead nurturing program without a buyer's journey map is like going on a road trip without any directions. It's slow going, it can be treacherous and it's definitely not the fastest route to your destination. This aimless plan will cost you a lot of money and time in the long run. If you take time to map typical buyer steps, you'll see natural places for aligning content to interest.

A. **Triggers:** Start by considering what triggers an investment in your solution. Make sure the triggers you select are repeatable by a segment of buyers, and hopefully something you can identify.

B. **Segments:** Next, identify which of your buyer segments are likely to encounter this trigger.

C. **Questions:** Last, identify what questions your buyers will want to answer in each stage of the journey. I've provided some generic questions in the sample below, but you will want to get very specific to your organization.

Later in Chapter 11 we'll explore how to map offers to align with buyer questions.

Audience	Purchase Trigger	Stage of Buying Cycle	Questions	Offers
Profile 1	Purchase Trigger #1	Problem Identification	What are my peers who are most effective doing? What trends are hot in my industry? How do I compare to my peers?	
		Solution Evaluation	How can I address this challenge? What is the difference in costs for the various approaches? What will I need to address this challenge a year from now? Which vendors offer the features that are important for my business? Who like me has each vendor worked with?	
		Vendor Comparison	Do they have a good reputation for support after purchase? Has my sales person been responsive? Do I feel important to this vendor?	
		Negotiation	How do I build a business case for budget approval? Will this vendor be the best long term choice? What references can I speak with?	
Profile 2	Purchase Trigger #2	Problem Identification		
		Solution Evaluation		
		Vendor Comparison		
		Negotiation		
Profile 1&2	Purchase Trigger #3	Problem Identification		
		Solution Evaluation		
		Vendor Comparison		
		Negotiation		
Profile 3	Purchase Trigger #4	Problem Identification		
		Solution Evaluation		
		Vendor Comparison		
		Negotiation		

For example, if I were marketing plows to commercial property managers, the purchase triggers and questions might look like this:

Purchase Trigger	Problem Identification Questions
Heavy snow weather forecast for the entire winter season	○ Will the projected snowfall occur in a small number of large storms, or in many small storms?
	○ Is snow expected to be accompanied by ice and wind or mild temperatures?
	○ Are other property management companies soliciting my customers with promises of new equipment?
	○ In heavy snowfall scenarios how quickly do commercial clients expect snow removal to occur?
	○ How can I assess whether my current equipment will be able to manage the expected workload?
	○ How much staff should I hire in preparation for the season?
Cost of fuel dropped more than $1/gallon	○ How are other commercial property management companies investing their fuel savings?
	○ How long are fuel prices expected to stay low?
	○ Are other property managers changing their prices based on dropping fuel costs?

2. First impressions are everything! How to create the critical first touch.

A potential buyer exchanged their email address by attending an event, watching an online video, or maybe downloading some content from your website. The bait you placed successfully engaged the audience, but what's next? The very next touch can either secure more trust, or permanently put your buyer back in their shell.

DON'T:

○ Send an asset that is unrelated to what they just consumed. If your buyer watched a web seminar on virtualization best practices, don't send information about backup and security, even if you offer both.

○ Assume they internalized the message of the content previously accessed—I promise they aren't as deeply wedded to your material as you.

○ Start pushing meetings or aggressive next steps that leapfrog their indicated stage.

DO:

- ❍ Reference the content they already consumed even if you are putting them into a programmed nurture stream.

- ❍ Make a reasonable guess about what they might want to read as follow-up from their first engagement. (Your buyer's journey map can illustrate this clearly).

- ❍ Select content that helps them implement an idea you shared in the previous content.

- ❍ Invite conversation by sharing contact details and communicating on behalf of real people at your company.

3. Plan your content marketing mix.

There is a plethora of research that shows people learn in different ways. Some are more visual, some auditory, some hands-on and others absorb best by reading. In fact, most of us retain information best with a combination of approaches. Lead nurturing is not about making a single, transient impression—it's about using content to help our buyers explore, evaluate and learn to trust our brand. The most effective programs don't do this via one "learning channel." Instead, they offer content across a variety of formats.

For example, instead of just sending out a PDF, drive your visitors to a landing page where that PDF resides, but also includes a video Q&A with the author and an interactive poll. You don't need to reinvent the wheel, simply repurpose existing content into fresh, new formats.

It takes more work to offer content across many mediums, but the extra time investment pays off with an increase in more qualified conversions and a more engaged audience.

4. Help buyers compare.

Sorry, marketers, it's not all about us, even while buyers are considering which solutions are best for them. Those of us with complex offerings are very good at talking about our solution. The problem arises when we forget our buyers' need more than just information about what we do. They need information that helps them compare the benefits of our solution to the alternative. I don't just mean competing options, I mean also explaining why our solution is a better choice than doing nothing at all. Buyers need information that helps them build a justification for parting with their hard-earned budget.

Comparison documents, reviews, evaluation checklists, and ROI calculators, for example, are much more valuable than product data sheets and specifications alone. These are the real tools that help your buyer feel good about making a decision to purchase your solution.

5. Establish lead nurturing success metrics.

There are plenty of industry statistics about what is average, or best-case metrics for lead nurturing programs, but in the early stages of your program you should build a baseline and measure success against yourself. Look for measurable improvements over time and set both short-term and long-term goals.

A. Email open rates — What percentage of your audience opened each email campaign? While there is probably a cap to how large an open rate can be in practice, your goal should be to see open rates continually improve as the campaign progresses. If this happens, it is a good sign that your message is relevant and your audience is properly targeted. It's also important to evaluate open rates by segment, and not simply the aggregate score. Is one group underperforming? Does one audience respond better than another? What content is resonating with which audience?

B. Offer downloads — Building compelling content and calls-to-action are critical to the success of a nurturing program. Tracking who is accessing that content is necessary, but raw numbers don't tell the entire story. As offers are presented throughout the campaign, are individuals taking more than one? Do they stop acting at a certain spot? How does one offer pickup relate to another? Does subject line affect offer download rate?

C. List quality —Throughout the course of the campaign, the quality of your database should be improving. You should be able to collect new information about the interests of the people in the database on the basis of what they consume, and the use of form fields when accessing your content. In addition, bounce rates should be declining as you remove bad email addresses from the database. List quality is a constant challenge that never goes away, but you should see improvements over time.

D. Unsubscribe rates — Don't be afraid of unsubscribes! Accept the fact that members of your audience will unsubscribe from your communications, proving you are narrowing down your list to people truly interested in hearing from you. However, you do need to monitor for spikes or unusual behavior. The frequency of your communications often affects unsubscribe rates as much as the content of those communications. Keep monitoring, and look for patterns of change.

E. Social shares — If the content you are presenting is really good, your partners and prospective customers will want to share it. Are you seeing links to the content being tweeted? Does someone post it to a LinkedIn Group? Have you been able to leverage it within a blog post? Social shares by themselves are not the goal of the nurturing program, but it is a helpful way to identify the impact of your message.

F. Event participation — While most of the nurturing campaign is electronic in nature, there are physical as well as virtual events built into the program. While it's important to understand the volume of attendees, you should also actively understand participation by engagement. How engaged are individuals who attend your events? Do they ask good questions? Are they raising their hand for follow-up? Do they stay on for the entire session? Are session evaluations pointing to a positive experience? Do they come back for subsequent events? These are the type of participation goals that nurturing programs must measure.

G. Downstream impact — Over the long term, the effect of lead nurturing will be directly related to critical business impact metrics such as revenue contribution, length of sales cycle and win rate. As a next step, build an attribution model within your marketing system to measure how each activity is influencing the long-term growth of the organization.

CHAPTER 10

Personas, Not Profiles

- 71% of companies that **exceed revenue and lead goals** have documented personas vs. 37% that simply meet goals and 26% that miss them[17]

- Marketers who use personas and map content to the buyer's journey enjoy 73% **higher conversions** from response to marketing-qualified lead (MQL)[18]

- Customer-centric companies are 60% **more profitable** than non–customer centric organizations[19]

Now that I have your attention, let's start with the basics. What the heck is a persona? Personas are fictional representations of people who interact with your company and offerings. A persona is a composite of market research and remind us of the human element of our target audience. We give them a name, a personality and use them to visualize who buys and uses our services. Some people refer to personas as psychographic summaries of your audience.

Yuck! TMMS. (Too much marketing speak!) Let's drop the jargon and put context around this definition.

---

17 Source: Understanding B2B Buyers Benchmark Study

18 Source: Aberdeen Research http://www.aberdeenessentials.com/cmo-essentials/stop-trying-find-easy-way-build-buyer-persona/

19 Source: Deloitte and Touche

I'd like to introduce you to Anne. My grandmother Anne loved to cook, was fabulous at arts and crafts, and served on the school committee well after her children were out of the house. She lived in Connecticut with her husband and tiny dog, Snowball. Sounds pretty typical, right? That's Anne's profile. Most marketers do a good job of understanding these general characteristics of their audience.

But there was a lot more to Anne than that. While she loved her grandchildren fiercely, her world revolved around her schedule. Even when she was asking about our recent accomplishments, she was thinking about how it would impact her day. Who could she brag to about what happened? Would she need to take time out of her schedule to celebrate?

While she slaved over the stove and her magical cooking, she'd scold you if you even thought about eating anything before dinner and ruined your appetite for "her meal." She was a quick learner who picked up how to use a computer in her 70s so she could leave her recipes as a legacy to her family when she was gone. The best way to get Anne's attention was to challenge her. She never backed down from a fight and was a strong mama bear who protected her family, even when she was defending them from one of her own!

This was Anne's persona. To know Anne, and to market to her, you needed to understand more than that she had grandchildren, lived in the suburbs and was a good cook. You needed to know she was strong, focused on her needs as much as on those she loved, and never backed down from a fight.

The same applies to our target buyers, especially if you sell to other businesses. Assuming all IT managers or CPAs are the same doesn't make any more sense than saying all grandmothers are the same.

Personas help us break this cycle. They give us a way to group people who have the same role into segments that have shared psychographic attributes so we can market to them in a way that makes an emotional connection, not just a logical appeal. They allow us to be more relevant, and see better results.

Persona-based marketing is the difference between using a caricature of what a grandmother is supposed to be and truly getting to know the Grannie Annies of the world.

Grannie Annie

PROFILE	PERSONA
Contact profile data:	Top priorities
Title/Role	Most proud achievements
Geographic location	Biggest regrets
Education	Fears and frustrations
Income level	Obstacles
	Buying preferences
Business profile data:	Propensity to buy
Industry	Personality insights
Size of company (employees, revenue, # of customers)	
Headquarters location	
Public vs. private	
Years in business	

We document our personas and give them names not to be clever or cute—but to remind ourselves that we are targeting real human beings. Personas allow us to create an identity which can guide everything that we do, from building new products and capabilities to writing advertising copy.

Persona Optimization Framework

Some organizations are just getting started with personas. Others have built fully realized personas and are using them strategically. To help clarify the different stages of maturity as it relates to persona development and use, I'm going to reference the Persona

Optimization Framework.[20] The framework was developed based on an evaluation of more than 100 organizations where we compared the processes of those that reported they either exceeded, met or missed revenue and lead goals. I want to thank my friends at Cintell for sponsoring the benchmark study and research on which the framework is designed.

The framework has four stages of optimization.

1. Experimenting — Organizations in the experimenting stage have no dedicated resources or budget allocated to personas but have begun to explore their potential. Partially documented personas may exist, but they were developed based mostly on internal insights (e.g., the existing opinion of a sales or marketing team) and have limited usage across the organization. In this phase, personas resemble profiles and require a significant amount of research to flesh out further.

2. Emerging — Organizations fall into the emerging stage if they have committed to a persona project and assigned at least temporary resources to it. In this stage, organizations have typically started the persona effort by capturing research through qualitative interviews, assembling external research, and conducting some training on the use of personas with their sales and marketing teams.

3. Advancing — Advancing organizations have begun to embed personas into the ongoing process of the business. Personas are fully documented, budget is allocated to them, and individuals are held accountable for executing persona research. Both qualitative and quantitative research is completed at least once a year and personas are utilized by multiple parts of the organization—likely sales, marketing, and product development.

4. Fully Optimized — Although most organizations have not fully optimized their use of personas, there are many things we can learn from those that have reached their full potential. Fully optimized teams systematically update personas at least twice a year, have comprehensive training programs and heavily utilize personas across virtually all aspects of the business.

---

20 http://marketingadvisorynetwork.com/wp-content/uploads/2016/03/FINAL-Benchmark-Study-Understanding-Buyers-2016-Cintell-2.pdf

Each stage takes into account the critical areas of planning and resourcing, using, creating and maintaining personas. As you assess your organization you may find you have strengths in one category, and areas to mature in others. That's perfectly normal and will provide you direction on where to invest next.

Try to avoid the temptation to consider this a step model. While it's unlikely an organization will go from zero to fully optimized in one phase, it is not necessary to progress slowly from one stage to another. Consider your goals and seek to gain support for the highest commitment possible. Those organizations that are advancing or fully optimized gain the greatest rewards.

Three Essential Components of Personas: Creating, Using, and Maintaining

1. Creating personas

Although personas are different at each organization, there is a process and pattern to creating personas that work. You can't Google your way to persona greatness. Taking time to do primary research up front is essential to building personas that have an impact on your business.

When starting out, many people aren't clear about how many personas they need. There is no magic number, though the quantity does become apparent once the research is completed. Patterns will appear, allowing you to group your research into segments by what they have in common. Most single product/service companies have 3–5 primary personas that illustrate their buyer's process.

The best persona insights come after assessing data patterns you have available and interviewing 5-6 people from each of the various roles involved in the buying process. Be sure to pick individuals from a cross section of your target buyer community. Ideally you will include both customers and organizations that are not yet customers in the interview process.

Be sure to include representatives from the entire buyer committee:

- User — who does your service or product serve directly?
- Economic buyer — who is going to pay for your offering? Who has budget authority to place an order?
- Influencers — who else can influence the purchase process?

Below you will find two examples of this committee. Keep in mind that these are not final personas—this is a sample of targets you will interview to flesh out relevant personas.

B2B Example: Inventory Management Software

Role	Titles	Organizational Characteristics	Headquarters Location
User	Inventory manager, Operations director, Facilities manager, procurement specialist	○ 25–500 employees ○ Industry: Manufacturing, transportation, wholesale distribution, retail, automotive ○ At least 100 part numbers managed	North America Mexico Australia Western Europe
Economic Buyer	Director of operations		
Influencers	Chief operations officer, shipping coordinator, VP finance, Director of IT		

B2C Example: Pediatric Orthodontist

Role	Demographics	Other Characteristics
User	10–17-year-old boys and girls Lives within 20 mile radius	Has crooked teeth or problem bite
Economic Buyer	Parents, Legal guardians	Has dental insurance or budget over $3,500
Influencers	Dental hygienist, primary dentist, grandparents, primary care physician	Office takes the same insurance(s) as orthodontist office

There's a direct correlation between conducting interviews and getting results. When you start to plan our out your interviews, you may feel overwhelmed. Conducting a handful of interviews feels manageable, but conducting 20, 30 or more can be intimidating. Don't be tempted to take a short cut. In our study, a full 70% of those who missed revenue and lead goals did not conduct qualitative interviews, compared to more than 80% of those who exceeded goals.

> 70% of companies who missed revenue and lead goals **did not** conduct qualitative persona interviews.

Use of qualitative interviews
(both customer & non-customer)

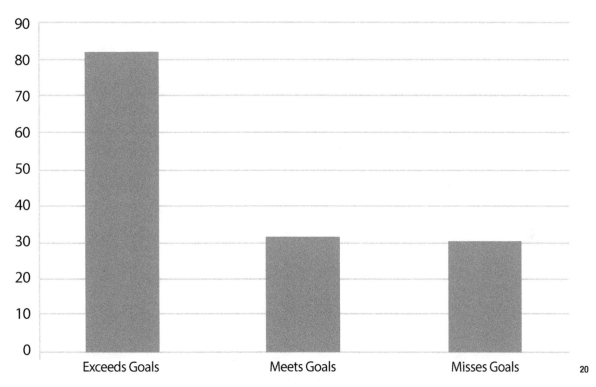

Qualitative research is the most time-consuming and richest part of the research process, but it should not be your only source of insight. Those who are most successful use a wide range of inputs including competitive analysis, surveys, internal staff interviews, external research and CRM data.

Start by evaluating your current persona creation services. Review each of the categories below to identify where on the optimization framework your practices fall. Be honest with yourself so you can identify areas to prioritize future investment.

Questions to benchmark yourself against the Optimization Framework:

- How are qualitative interviews conducted?
- Who do you survey?
- How diverse is the data you use to complete analysis?
- How complete is your industry research?
- How many personas has your organization developed?
- How complete are your personas?

Persona Optimization Framework
Creating Personas

CREATING	Fully Optimized	Advanced	Emerging	Experimenting
How are qualitative interviews conducted?	A regular cadence of qualitative interviews dedicated to persona research are conducted with both customers and non-customers	A regular cadence of qualitative interviews dedicated to persona research are conducted with both customers and non-customers	Small number of qualitative interviews conducted primarily with clients at the initial stage of persona research. Heavy reliance on internal employee interviews	Persona attributes are compiled using existing content or internal stakeholder interviews
Who do you survey?	Survey tools are used to validate persona research for both customer and non-customer	Ad hoc surveys are used to validate persona work	Surveys are used to collect profile information from the existing customer or communities.	No external surveys are used although we might use lead database surveys to collect information from internal stakeholders
How diverse is the data you use to complete analysis?	In addition to internal CRM data insights, extensive external data sources are utilized to augment internal data - this might include personality attributes, professional details, social indicators, educational level, income, etc.	Regular leverage of internal CRM data with some external data sources are utilized to augment internal data - this might include membership, social indicators, education level, income, etc.	Only company level data is integrated from third parties with little or no systemic use of internal CRM data	No third party data is utilized and only cursory CRM data usage occurs to create personas
How complete is your industry research?	Both competitive and industry trend research is quarterly	Both competitive and industry trend research is conducted at least once a year or around new growth initiative	Review of competitor websites and publicly available industry research upon initial persona project, no systematic approach to maintaining	Some industry and competitor research conducted to validate internal beliefs
How many personas has your organization developed?	The full customer community is represented by persona for user, champion, economic buyer and influencers. This could mean four or more personas	Most of the customer community is represented by personas at least 2 of these groups (user, economic buyer, and influencers)	Only decision-maker personas are created	Ad hoc persona development that covers primary buyer only
How complete are your personas?	All or most of the following are included in personas: demographic information, role in the buying process, buying preferences, hobbies and interests, organizational goals and priorities, drivers and motivators, fears and challenges, assocations, content topic preferences, KPI/Success metrics and personality traits	Most of the following are included in personas: demographic information, role in the buying process, buying preferences, hobbies and interests, organizational goals and priorities, drivers and motivators, fears and challenges, associations, content topic preferences, KPI/Success metrics and personality traits	Personas go beyond demographic information to include organizational goals, priorities and fears	Personas are mostly profiles of key demographic information with perhaps a smattering of goals and challenges

2. Using personas

Building personas is a lot of work, but the results of your efforts can be used to improve results across multiple areas of the business. Make sure you capitalize on your persona insights across the organization.

- ○ Sales training — Next to marketing, sales will feel an almost immediate benefit of better understanding their potential customers, but don't assume they will know how to use them. Training is essential.

- ○ Messaging — Knowing your audience makes developing messaging infinitely easier and more effective. Persona research will uncover what pain points, word choices, and more will resonate with your audience(s) so you can adjust tone, value statements and content priorities.

- ○ Product development — Whether you offer a product or service, your customers are looking for something of value from you. By understanding them, your professional services and engineering/development teams can produce products that are more likely to be adopted and used. In fact, persona-driven product development leads to 10–20% higher customer satisfaction levels.[21]

- ○ Customer support — Don't overlook customer support. They interact with your customers every day and live and breathe your brand promise to each customer they interact with. Teach them to understand who's on the other end of the phone so they can respond not just with answers, but with an emotional and empathetic connection.

- ○ Executive decision makers — The organizations that embrace personas most effectively have buy-in from their executive team, who reference personas in meetings from the board room to the lunchroom.

- ○ Designer inspiration — While personas don't replace the need for brand guidelines, they do provide insight that designers can leverage to create resonance visually with your target audience. Share personas with agencies and consultants who are stewards of your brand.

- ○ Demand generation — The principles of loss aversion tell us that buyers are more likely to move away from pain than move toward potential gain. This means in your

---

21 http://pragmaticmarketing.com/resources/the-roi-of-being-market-driven

demand generation efforts, you've got to directly address what is causing your buyer the most pain, today. Persona research uncovers this pain, allowing you to align lead generation campaigns to tap into their desires, not just their pocket books.

○ Database segmentation — This is perhaps the most overlooked aspect of persona marketing. Your personas should form the foundation for how you segment your marketing messages, beginning with your addressable database. Start by tagging your contacts with a relevant persona. Take the time to consider priorities, motivators and personality attributes, not just title. Need a little motivation? Those organizations that exceed both lead and revenue goals are more than three times as likely to segment their database by persona-related fields as those that meet or miss them.

○ External agency briefings — Your external agencies will never know your business as well as you do, but you can jump-start their effectiveness by sharing your persona research. The more they understand your buyer, the better they can serve your needs.

Questions to benchmark yourself against the Optimization Framework:

○ Which departments understand and leverage your personas in their day-to-day work?

○ Are you effective at mapping contacts to personas?

○ For what percentage of your database have you identified a correlating persona?

○ Who is your executive sponsor?

Tip: Increase adoption of personas across the business

Looking to transform personas into a companywide motivator instead of a marketing initiative?

○ Put cutouts of your persona around the office with related quotes

○ Refer to the personas by name when making decisions—i.e., when asking for a new product feature, product management should ask, "Who is this for?"

○ Bring in your personas for the company to meet—feature real-world inspiration

○ Host lunch-and-learns across the business

○ Integrate into new hire training

○ Incentivize your sales team to offer feedback to help keep personas up-to-date

---

Persona Optimization Framework
Using Personas

USING	Fully Optimized	Advanced	Emerging	Experimenting
How well does your organization use personas?	Personas are utilized across the entire business including sales training, messaging, product development, customer support, executive decision making, designer inspiration, demand generation and external agency briefings	Personas are utilized across most of the business including at least four of these areas: sales training, messaging, product development, customer support, executive decision making, demand generation and external agency briefings	Personas are utilized for marketing messaging and sales training, with ad hoc use across product development or other departments.	Personas are utilized for marketing messaging, but nowhere else in the organization
How effectively do you segment your database by persona?	Comprehensive database mapping using progressive profiling, demographic information and content signals	Database mapped by demographic information and maintained using either content signals or survey data	One-time database mapping exercise completed. No systematic approach to maintain it. Based on demographic information (title, industry, company size) only	Program-specific list pulls by demographic information (title, industry, company size)
How much of your database contains a persona attribute?	90%+ of the customer database is mapped by persona and 50%+ of the prospect database has an identified persona attached to each record	At least half of the prospect and customer database has a persona attribute on each contact record	Less than 50% but more than 10% of the database has been mapped	The database contains a field for "persona" which is used ad hoc. Less than 10% of the database is mapped to a
Which executives sponsor your persona work?	There is executive sponsorship from the CEO. Although the CMO is the primary sponsor, each member of the executive committee has assigned leaders on their team to ensure that personas are utilized across the organization	CMO takes on leadership role with personas being a formal part of the charter for marketing with support from stakeholders in sales and product.	Line of business or director of marketing sponsors persona initiative with support from stakeholders in sales	Line of business or director of marketing sponsors persona initiative

3. Maintaining personas

Personas are not a one-and-done initiative. Often, this is where many organizations struggle to continually realize value from their investment in persona research. Once you publish your personas, it's tempting to check them off the to-do list and move on. However, markets change. Our buyers evolve. New priorities appear, new economic conditions emerge and who we target changes over time. Building a sustainable process is critical to long-term impact.

While personas don't need to be updated every day, the highest-performing companies systematically validate and update their segments every six months. More volatile industries such as technology may warrant more frequent updates. Organizations with longer sales cycles within slower-moving industries may warrant less.

Whatever your cadence, I have found there are multiple sources of insight available to help keep personas up-to-date. Your sales team is a constant source of customer insight. The aggregate results of campaigns in whichever email or marketing automation system you deploy can dictate which topics are top-of-mind and resonating, and which are growing stale. Third-party research can aid you in keeping tabs on what's changing in the world of your buyers. As with persona creation, however, ongoing persona maintenance is best conducted by including additional qualitative research. In our framework, fully optimized organizations not only systematically update personas, they validate insights on an ongoing basis using a multitude of sources.

Changing and publishing new persona versions can quickly become a version control issue. I recommend storing personas in easily accessible online collaboration tools or the company intranet. Finding personas is half the battle for your employees using them, and storing them digitally (rather than in printed format) allows you to update them with ease.

Questions to benchmark yourself against the Optimization Framework:

o   How often do you update your personas?

o   Where do you store them?

o   Do you leverage third-party data to maintain personas over time?

Persona Optimization Framework
Maintaining Personas

MAINTAINING	Fully Optimized	Advanced	Emerging	Experimenting
How often do you update your personas?	Systematically updated at least once every 6 months and as part of any new growth initiative	Updated at least once a year and as part of any new growth initiative	Updated every 1 - 2 years	Updated as part of a one-time strategic shift (new leadership, new offer launch, etc.)
Where do you store your personas?	Personas are made easily accessible via online collaboration tools that are kept current, along with on-demand training modules	Personas are made easily accessible via online collaboration tools such as Sharepoint, Chatter or intranet	Personas are stored in static documents e.g. PDF or PowerPoint	Formal personas are not documented
Do you have a process to use data to maintain personas over time?	In addition to internal CRM data insights, extensive external data sources are utilized to augment internal data - this might include personality attributes, membership, social indicators, education level, income, etc.	Regular leverage of internal CRM data with some external data sources are utilized to augment internal data - this might include personality attributes, membership, social indicators, education level, income, etc.	Only company level data is integrated from third parties, with little or no systematic use of internal CRM data	No third party data is utilized and only cursory CRM data usage occurs

CASE STUDY: MORE THAN MEETS THE EYE

I recently engaged with a client that was launching a service focused on serving the recruiting industry. My specific deliverable was to build a messaging platform for the company, and as part of my standard process I requested to speak with customers and prospects to understand their challenges, pain points, and other critical persona insights. My client was excited to jump into the messaging project, but they were exceptionally reluctant to set up these interviews for me. I was surprised.

Although clearly laid out as a requirement in my statement of work, and despite a handful of conversations about how to engage, the interview portion of my project remained at a standstill. I called a meeting to understand their hesitation and try to move beyond this roadblock. In the meeting, my client revealed the motivation behind their reluctance. They felt that any conversations with customers or prospects that didn't have the end goal of making a sale was a wasted opportunity. They wanted me to simply write the messaging without conducting the interviews. In their words, "We trust you, Samantha, you have worked with recruiters before, just write what you think they care about."

While their blind trust was flattering, it was completely flawed. Yes, I had worked with recruiters before, and yes, I had an idea of what was important to this profession in general. But for this client, I implored, there would be specific challenges and variations in the types of recruiters we targeted that would dictate what messages were appropriate for them. Every time I complete persona interviews, even for industries I know well, I learn something new in the context of the business I am supporting. Their assumption, that all recruiters are made equal, is common. Their unspoken bias that I may have known everything about their buyers already is equally common, which is what makes persona research so effective. It can be a major competitive advantage to be armed with the insight of your buyers ahead of product or messaging launches.

Additionally, I reminded my client that their relationship with customers was not solely for the purpose of selling to them. Conducting persona research gives someone an opportunity to vent, to describe their problems, and to tell you about themselves. It's easier than you think to get someone to open up, and it helps communicate a brand promise that my client was customer-focused enough to take the time to ask. Eventually, I convinced my client to secure the necessary interviews.

The organization was surprised by the insights we gained. Rather than simply clean up what they had written previously, we uncovered some messaging points that needed a pretty complete shift, something that would not have been discovered otherwise until well after the messaging went live. It's a lot less expensive to change the messaging *before* the campaign launches.

In this example, I was able to hold firm in my convictions and not fall into the trap of writing without doing the research, because I learned this lesson years ago.

CASE STUDY: ALL EXCHANGE ADMINISTRATORS ARE CREATED EQUAL (OR ARE THEY?)

At the time, I was running marketing campaigns that influenced MS Exchange Administrators. These were the people who managed email systems on behalf of their businesses. I'd been working in the information technology sector for a long time and I was pretty sure I understood this audience. They were mostly men in their mid-thirties, technically-oriented, and science fiction lovers who understood the nuances of the differences between Star Wars and Star Trek with the same ferocious conviction as a Red Sox fan knows his team versus the Yankees.

It would have been very easy to consider our persona work done given my experience. But it would have been a huge mistake. Prior to this engagement, the marketing organization had treated all Exchange Administrators in their database the same—with a single nurture stream of messages. This one-size-fits-all approach meant our email open rates, event registration numbers and content downloads had supported the rapidly growing business, but had recently seen flat performance. In the previous year, no measurable improvements in conversion had been made despite a growing database of prospects.

My peers in the global marketing team set out to discover why this had happened. After conducting many qualitative interviews and looking at content download patterns, something really important emerged. We realized that all Exchange Administrators were not the same.

To you, reading a chapter about personas, this isn't really all that shocking. But to a business that had relied on an incorrect assumption that they understood their audience, the revelation was critically important.

Going into the research we had a hypothesis that the industry the administrator worked in mattered to the appropriate messaging. What we learned was that it didn't matter very much. What *did* matter was their primary mission orientation, and what role email played in their priorities and objectives day-to-day.

While all Exchange Administrators had virtually the same series of tasks related to managing email servers, this audience was in fact segmented into three types of exchange administrators.[22]

Exchange Administrator Personas

Persona	Common Traits (Profile)	Distinct Characteristics
Steve — The multitasker	○ Reports to Director of IT ○ Held the same job for 5+ years ○ Gadget lover ○ Microsoft Exchange certified ○ Primary job is to ensure that the business has no disruption to its email service by maintaining a secure and available email server(s) ○ Knows how to troubleshoot but has few if any coding skills ○ Takes more complaints than compliments and has grown used to being the butt of his business partners' jokes	Running the email server is just one of Steve's many responsibilities. He has general network responsibility that includes the website, intranet services and other network appliances. Email is more important to the employees than to him personally and his email responsibilities often interrupt his other responsibilities. He knows just enough to do his job but has no passion for email management.
Dan — The protector		Dan considers email a secondary driver; his real passion is security. He's terrified of a data breach and spends most of his time studying hacker protocols and the latest virus signatures.
Robert — The governor		Governance is Robert's primary driver. He sees himself less a part of IT and more a partner with the compliance team on a mission to make sure all policies are followed. He believes every email is the company's property and protects it as if it were his own.

This example illustrates the importance of going beyond profile-level information to understand the deeper insights behind the demographics.

Following this research, we developed segmented lead nurturing programs along with new sales training. As a result, email conversion rates improved by more than 20%, putting more qualified leads into the pipeline and fueling the marketing engine for growth.

---

22 I've changed the name of the personas to protect the privacy of this organization.

HOW-TO GUIDELINES: CONDUCT INSIGHTFUL QUALITATIVE INTERVIEWS

I hope I've convinced you that qualitative research is an essential part of your persona journey. In this section, I'm going to outline everything you need to excel at it. Much of this section I developed in conjunction with Cintell for the Ultimate Guide to Conducting Insightful Persona Interviews.[23] It's been road-tested within dozens of persona projects in addition to my own work, and I hope it helps you tap into the true voice of your customers.

Step #1: Prepare an interview guide

Before scheduling any interviews you'll want to develop an interview guide. While the guide should not be a rigid script, it is an extremely useful tool for fostering a quality conversation.

Using a variety of questions spurs the most insightful discussions that can later be used to find patterns. Each interview should comprise five parts:

1. Organizational Context
2. Personality Attributes
3. Propensity to Buy and Purchase Preferences
4. Motivators and Priorities
5. Content Clues

Below are a series of sample questions broken down by section that you can use to build your interview guide. You likely won't have time to use all of these in each interview; instead, select 1–2 questions from each section that you feel will best match the cadence of your conversation. They are designed to solicit discussion and identify patterns, and you should customize them for your business.

> Let the natural conversation flow as it does. If the customer is passionate about a particular topic, it signals something of critical importance. Let them talk so as not to miss out on critical insights.

---

23 http://marketingadvisorynetwork.com/wp-content/uploads/2016/03/FINAL-Persona-Interview-Guide-Cintell.pdf

Organizational Context

I like to start with these questions because it warms up the discussion by putting the participant at ease. It's a great way to build rapport with the interviewee. That's not to suggest you should think of these as throwaway questions. Takeaways will come not only from the responses you receive but also from the tone in which the question is answered.

For example, the two responses below give the same answer, but the context is significantly different.

QUESTION: Who does the grocery shopping in your household?

RESPONSE A: I do all the grocery shopping. I bring a list of recipes so I can browse the store and be inspired for dinner this week. Sometimes I lose track of time.

RESPONSE B: (Sighs) I do all the grocery shopping. I bring a list so I can get in and out of the store as fast as possible.

In both examples the answer was the same, but the tone (and what you learning from it) is completely different. Responder A loves the grocery store. She's inspired by walking the aisles and thinks of it as "me time." Responder B hates grocery shopping and thinks of it as a chore.

Can you imagine the different messages and offers you might provide for one versus the other?

QUESTION BANK

- ○ What was the best team experience you've ever been a part of? Explain why.
- ○ Put yourself back in the classroom. What grade would you give your current (insert relevant process, category, or role)_____? (If they didn't give it an A, ask as follow-up what would it take to get it one grade higher.)
- ○ How is your team structured? What is the title of the person you report to at work?
- ○ What's the most frustrating part of your day?
- ○ How long have you been in your current job?
- ○ How much would you spend without checking with someone else?

Tip: On rare occasions an interviewee isn't comfortable answering one of your questions. Give them permission to pass, but remind them that this is for market research only—it's totally confidential and none of their responses will be aligned to them or their organization. Often, after you confirm that the data won't be used for other purposes they will open up.

Propensity to Buy

The persona interview is not the time to evaluate specific features of your offering; however, you can gain important sentiment insight into how your audience prioritizes the category of offerings.

QUESTION BANK

I'm going to read a series of statements and pause after each one. I'd like you to tell me whether you strongly agree, somewhat agree, somewhat disagree or strongly disagree with the statement.

My [CATEGORY]_____ is easy to use
_____ is my most critical concern
Our organization is not willing to invest in _____ that I trust
The fear of losing _____keeps me up at night
Most _____ could meet my needs
Price is the most important factor in selecting _____
Easy of use is the most critical component of _____
I'm likely to change our current _____
I focus heavily on _____
I have at least one _____ I couldn't live without
I am very effective at _____
A significant factor of my success is my ability to _____
It is hard to find _____ when I need it
I feel confident _____ will deliver on my goals

What percentage of your budget are you allocating to each of the following:

Category	% of this year's budget	How does this relate to last year? (Increase, decrease, no change)	How do you expect to change in the next year? (Increase, decrease, no change)
Category 1			
Category 2			
Category 3			
....			

- When was the last time you purchased (category of offering)? Describe the process to me. What triggered you to make the purchase?
  - If you had to choose between two _____ that did the same thing, what criteria would you use to choose one over the other?
  - How did you decide which offerings to evaluate?
  - Who else was involved in the purchase process?
  - If two providers had equivalent services, how would you decide which product to select?
- Who do you consult when spending $X?
- What was the best purchase process you ever participated in? Describe why.
- When a new gadget comes out that you might want to use, you are most likely to:
  - (a) Stand in line for hours to be the first in your network to have one
  - (b) Place a pre-order, excited to be among early owners but not willing to wait in line
  - (c) Sit back and wait for version 2, so all the kinks will be worked out

Personality Attributes

Although we're focused on business-related insights that can be applied to real tactical execution, don't be tempted to skip this section. While it probably doesn't matter if your interviewee is a cat or dog person (unless you own a pet store), it is critical that you understand how they think. These questions will help you build an emotional, not just logical, connection with your buyer.

QUESTION BANK

- ○ Who is a personal hero of yours?

- ○ How would your peers describe you?

- ○ What would your work colleagues be surprised to learn about you?

- ○ What was the last book you didn't finish? What prevented you from finishing it?

- ○ If you could have any superpower you could imagine, what would it be? Why?

- ○ If the "voice in your head" giving you advice was a cartoon character, who would it be? (For the record, mine would be Velma from *Scooby-Doo*, but I don't always listen to her.)

- ○ What brands do you admire? Why

- ○ When deciding to spend $500, you are most likely to (pick one):

  - o Carefully evaluate all my options using a spreadsheet to weigh them

  - o Whip out the debit card and ask questions later

  - o Consult with my network to verify the quality of my options

Motivators and Priorities

Understanding what is important to your buyer is essential to building an offering that is compelling. When this portion of a persona is well researched it's easy to go through a list of all your benefits and capabilities and select the value messages that are most likely to resonate for a particular audience.

QUESTION BANK

- ○ What are you most proud of achieving in the last 12 months?

- ○ What's the hardest part of your job?

- ○ What are your top four priorities for this year?

- ○ When you look back 18 months from now, how will you know you've been successful?

- ○ What have you most regretted not doing in the past six months?

Content Clues

One of the most immediate values a persona can provide is to offer guidance on the type of content that will attract your audience. In this section you'll test a series of ideas. While you may find specific pieces to produce, the purpose of this exercise is to identify topics of interest and to test how your audience responds to different formats such as a how-to guide or a research report.

QUESTION BANK

I'm going to share a series of headlines. After each one I will pause, and I'd like you to rate on a 0-to-5 scale how compelled you would be to read an article with that headline.

> 0—not at all interested

> 5—would drop what I'm doing right now to read it

Title	Rating
"How to _____"	
"Everything You Ever Wanted to Know about _____ but Were Afraid to Ask"	
"10 Reasons to _____"	
"Cost-Effective_____"	
"Getting Started with _____"	
"Eight Ways You're Doing _____ Wrong"	
"Does Your _____ Pass the Quality Test?"	
"5 Signs It's Time to ..."	
"Quantifying the Value of _____"	
"Six Ways to _____"	

The title prompts above I've found effective and easy to apply to most businesses. The blanks should be completed with topics related to the key capabilities of your offering. However, don't limit yourself to these specific frameworks—pull additional ideas from Google keyword research, your existing lead nurturing campaigns, and ideas generated by your sales and product teams. You'll be surprised when conducting the research how one persona will be drawn to one set of titles, and another to totally different selections.

This part of the interview should be highly dynamic. If you're not finding content that entices (4s and 5s), throw in a new title based on your discussion. You may even want to pause and ask what they searched for last week but couldn't find.

QUESTION BANK

- What was the last book you read for pleasure? What was the last professional book you read?
- What publications/magazines do you read regularly?
- For what keywords do you have saved searches?
- What was the last professional event you attended?
- Do you belong to any professional associations? Which?
- If I were to look at your Google search history, what would be the headlines of the last three articles you read related to (insert category)?

Step #2: Recruit candidates.

At this point all your hard work is about to pay off. You're probably chomping at the bit to get started but wondering how to recruit the right candidates.

Unfortunately, there is no magic bullet for recruiting interview targets, but there are some tried-and-true techniques. You'll be surprised how many people agree to participate when you take the time to ask.

To Incent or Not to Incent

The decision to provide financial incentives for interview participation is based on the size and willingness of your audience to participate in the interview process. Although not always necessary, I use a financial incentive in about 75% of the interviews I conduct.

Participant Profile	Incentive Value
Consumer/User	$25
Manager	$50–$100
Executive	$200–$300

If you have the time and relationships to recruit candidates without offering an incentive I encourage you to do so—but don't save the money at the expense of objectivity. Be sure you are recruiting participants who truly represent your audience, not interviewees who are selected because they are more readily available.

Now that you know who your targets are, and what you want to ask, it's time to start scheduling interviews. Your database and social media tools like LinkedIn InMail are both good recruiting tools. If you have a particularly challenging audience to recruit, or simply don't have time to schedule the interviews yourself, there are reputable services that can help. Make sure you don't just pick any calling service—choose one that has a track record for research recruitment.

Step #3: Conduct the interview.

Finally the time has come for you to start interviewing. Take a deep breath, get your glass of water ready and shut down everything except for your notebook and conference calling line to avoid distractions. Persona interviews deserve your undivided attention.

○ First and foremost, remember this is *not* a survey—this is a conversation. Don't be a slave to your interview guide. Don't be afraid to skip a question, or dig deeper to understand something further. Add a new question if the one you asked isn't getting to the heart of what you want to address.

○ Make your interview candidate feel comfortable right from the start. Welcome them by name and thank them for joining you. Remind them this is purely for market research and all their responses will be kept confidential. (Remember this conversation should not be used to qualify them for a sales call.) Be sure to ask if they have any questions before you get started.

○ Although it is tempting to solicit product-specific win/loss or feature feedback, the persona interview is not the time to ask those questions. If you can't help yourself, reserve those questions for the end so as not to bias your interviewee's responses to your primary goal, persona questions.

○ Silence can be your friend. Don't try to fill every pause in the conversation. The quiet will encourage your interview candidate to drive deeper into their thoughts.

○ Sometimes the best insights start as a passing comment. When you hear something you'd like to learn more about, simply ask for more details. "Could you tell me more about XYZ?" leaves room for the interviewee to dig deeper.

○ Use the interviewee's first name throughout the interview. It shows you are listening and that you value their opinion.

○ Plan in advance how you are going to document the information collected. I like to type my notes and have a notebook handy for written scribbles. You can also record the session and have it transcribed later. If you chose to record the session be sure to seek permission from your guest, but set them at ease by explaining the recording is to make sure you don't miss any of their feedback.

Step #4: Document your insights.

Taking hours of interviews and turning them into digestible insights is not easy, but it is extremely rewarding. Keep these tips in mind so you don't pull out your hair in the process:

○ Read and reread all the interview notes before doing anything else! Trust me, it's worth the time. You'll start to mentally group individuals into logical personas.

○ Next, lay out the data into grids so you can see everything in one place and validate your initial gut reactions.

○ Group personas by common themes including specific motivators and priorities. You can use Excel to manage responses or print out persona feedback and use the ever-trustworthy highlighter.

○ It's okay to start with too many personas. As you review findings, seek to simplify persona segments by their most common attributes. A persona should be able to stand on its own, and be distinctly unique from other persona segments. If you keep too many variations, you'll have too many versions to be truly actionable.

HOW-TO GUIDELINES: QUANTITATIVE SURVEY VALIDATION

Quantitative, survey-based persona research can be a great way to validate your interview findings. Surveys can be used for two purposes:

1. Validating your findings across a larger sample of your target audience
2. Identifying who in your database should be tagged as which persona

PERSONAS, NOT PROFILES

It's best to pick a selection of questions you asked in the interview guide and translate them for survey usage. Unlike your interviews, survey validation is best implemented with multiple-choice questions, not open-ended inquiry. For example:

DON'T ask, "What are your top priorities?"

DO list the priorities you want to validate. "On a scale of 1 to 5 rate how much of a priority each of these is to your job." (1 means not at all important and 5 means my highest priority.)

DON'T ask, "What's the most frustrating part of your day?"

DO list a selection of frustrations from which they can choose the three most relevant to them.

DON'T ask, "If the voice in your head giving you advice was a cartoon character, who would it be?"

DO provide a list of cartoon characters you found in your interviews and ask them to select the one that most resonates with them.

The advent of low-cost online survey tools has unleashed a powerful resource for persona research. Once the cloaked domain of the statistically minded, surveys are now being used for an increasing number of different efforts. Unfortunately, many professionals have never designed a survey. The user experience drives little traction, or worse yet, the resulting data is not reliable. Here are some good rules of thumb to keep in mind before publishing your survey.

Don't assume buzzword compliance. Hopefully the audience you have selected for your survey is relevant to the research you want to conduct. But that does not mean they will interpret industry buzzwords the same way you intend them. I once was asked to complete a survey about generational differences in communication styles. As a mother and marketer I was well suited to be a survey participant. Unfortunately, the survey labeled each generation without explanation. Honestly, I can't remember if 18–24-year-olds are Millennials or Generation X, and as a result my responses became invalid. This is easy to fix—if you're not sure whether a term is industry-specific, ask a neighbor to proofread it! Err on the side of over-explanation. The worst that can happen is that your participants feel overeducated.

Always define your rating scale. Just because you ask someone to rank their results from 1 to 5 does not mean they will know you mean 1 is best and 5 is worst! If you are providing a scale, be clear about what it means. Unless you have a specific goal (such as capturing an NPS score) it's a best practice to use a 5-point rating scale for survey questions because it provides a range of responses that are easily interpreted by the survey respondent.

> NPS, or Net Promoter Score is a specific model for capturing customer satisfaction that is generally modeled on a 10-point scale.

Repeat instructions on each question. This is probably the most common mistake I see in surveys. Often, there are instructions for a question and perhaps even a rating scale, but it is provided only once. By the fourth question, respondents forgot what instructions they are supposed to be following. Don't expect total recall. A little repetition in a survey is smart.

Set expectations. "Please complete this short survey on governance policies for data retention" does not imply a 50-question survey on everything from data retention to fines for non-compliance. And yet, the mismatch is more common than you might imagine. Instead of a bait and switch, tell your participants up front what to expect from the survey so they can dedicate the right amount of time and energy to your fact gathering. I always advocated being very specific. Phrases like the following are helpful for setting expectations:

- This survey should take no longer than 20 minutes to complete.
- Please help us by responding to this 10-question survey.
- We value your time. We will ask you to complete 3 questions before entering the survey to make sure your background is a perfect fit for our research needs.

Match survey incentives to effort. Have you ever seen those tourist T-shirts that read, "My Grandma toured Italy and all I got was this lousy T-shirt"? Your respondent's time is very valuable and you don't want them to think of the survey as "the lousy T-shirt." If you are going to offer something in exchange for participation, I implore you to match incentives to the level of effort required to complete the survey. A $5 charitable donation, a related content asset, or a copy of the research findings might be a perfect match for a survey that takes 10 minutes to complete, but it won't be sufficient for longer surveys. Before offering an incentive, consider how much time and energy is required to complete the survey and make sure you have earned the right to ask for that time.

Don't forget to collect profile information. Sometimes blind surveys are acceptable. However, in most cases the data is most valuable when you know something about the person completing the survey. Make sure to validate relevant characteristics up front to give you plenty of options to later correlate the data in interesting ways.

CHAPTER 11

Closing the Buyer's Journey Gaps

When we've been in business for a long time it's easy to assume we understand how our buyers prefer to engage during the sales process. But the truth is, we know a lot less than we think. After all, we're only directly engaged with a buyer for a small portion of their journey.

There is a whole lot of purchase activity that happens without us. To name a few:

- Web searches that lead visitors to sites other than ours (I know, it hurts to think our customers don't only think of us, but it's true!)
- Conversations with peers
- Industry articles that talk about the issues we address
- Internal meetings to map out requirements
- Meetings where your champion coaxes for budget approval
- Workflow steps to set up a purchase requisition

No one's job is to buy our product or service, so all this and more happens during interrupted spurts when our buyers are doing their real job.

Understanding the full buyer's journey allows us to:

- Reduce the length of the buying process
- Improve our win rate

○ Drive higher campaign conversion rates

○ Cement a positive impression of our brand

Doesn't that sound ideal? Most organizations struggle to reach the ideal even when they have taken the time to map out their buyer's stages. The challenge arises when we overlay this goal with the organizational complexities of most businesses.

We often organize our companies around domain expertise that aligns to specific segments of the buyer's journey, such as operations for contract negotiation, sales for vendor comparisons and support for implementation. However, our buyers don't neatly align themselves with our internal structures and move back and forth between stages in a nonlinear fashion. In fact, prospects interact with our brand as a single entity; from the home page of our website to our hold music to pricing negotiations with sales—it's all one brand, no matter how we've structured our company.

How our customers buy is fundamentally different from how we organize. For many companies this conflict creates significant gaps.

Luckily, organizational structure doesn't have to negatively affect our buyers' experiences. Marketing can, and should, step up and take a leadership role across all six stages of the buying journey, holistically. This chapter will detail these stages individually, and present considerations for improving the customer experience within each one.

STAGE 1: THE PURCHASE TRIGGER

Marketers and sales teams often think that the buying process starts when the buyer begins to search for a solution to a problem, when, in fact, there is an underlying trigger event that occurs to illuminate the opportunity in the first place. Understanding this vital purchase trigger is not only insightful, it is a core foundation for your content marketing strategy, sales process, and messaging work. By deeply understanding what circumstances create the need or desire for your offerings, you can align content and messaging to attract buyers as their triggers is activated.

Consider a buying process in my household. I purchased an incline treadmill. It was a significant investment, and as you'd expect, it was not an impulse purchase. However, the trigger might not be something you'd guess. Instead of a New Year's resolution to get fit, or the desire to train for a marathon, the trigger was something totally different. My 12-year-old son suffered an injury to his back. As his physical therapy sessions wound down, we were concerned about maintaining strength and continuing to rebuild his stamina. The content I searched for to inform my decision was very different, with my injured 12-year-old in mind, from what it would have been if reaching personal fitness goals was my driver.

The same principal applies for business-to-business transactions. Even something like a bank loan can have highly variable motivators. For example, a business might be seeking a loan to:

- ○ Grow the business by adding new equipment or headcount
- ○ Fill a cash flow gap caused by an unexpected delay in delivering services
- ○ Pay for unanticipated legal fees or fines
- ○ Buy a partner out

The messaging you would use to attract someone looking to grow their business is very different from the offers you would present to someone short on cash. I recommend building content and messaging around your top three to five purchase triggers only. This allows you to align the majority of your audience to your biggest drivers without trying to take on too much and risk watering down your core value proposition.

Be sure not to guess. Even if you don't have the bandwidth to conduct full persona interviews right now, you should use survey techniques and ad hoc conversations with buyers to validate your assumptions about what triggers a purchase investigation.

STAGE 2: SOLUTION DISCOVERY

Once a triggering activity has occurred, it is likely that your buyer has many ways to fulfill their need. Case in point: I ended up purchasing a treadmill. However, we could have chosen to join a gym, extend physical therapy sessions, or seek out classes—all of which would have achieved the same goals.

At the solution discovery phase, your buyers are not yet considering specific vendors; rather, they are thinking about the variety of approaches they can take to address their underlying need.

- Do they want to build a solution themselves?
- Could they add more staff to address the gap?
- Perhaps there is a third-party service that competes with product offerings?

When I decided to freshen up my website I had several choices. I could purchase a template and edit it myself. I could hire a freelance web developer. I could subscribe to one of the many "website in a box" services that have popped up. And of course I could have partnered with an agency.

I considered a host of factors before deciding which avenue to pursue.

- How long will it take to execute each approach?
- Roughly how much will each cost my business?
- Will I have more control with one approach over another?
- What will be easiest to maintain over time?
- Do we have a corporate policy that would influence my decision? For example, does my business allow me to host certain types of data externally?

To serve buyers at this stage of their journey, your content should be focused on helping buyers weigh the pros and cons of various approaches, rather than talking about your specific offering. For example, I wasn't ready to talk about which web developer I would engage; I was simply narrowing down how I would approach the project. Of course, those that I found most insightful in helping me make this determination were top-of-mind for consideration when I decided to proceed to the next stage.

Keep in mind that while sometimes this decision is made before proceeding to the next stage (evaluation of options), it's not uncommon for the two stages to have some overlap. For this reason, make it easy for your prospective buyers to navigate to information related to vendor comparison from your solution approach materials. You can see in the two examples below that a simple callout box with links embedded in context is an easy and effective approach to execute.

At the end of this paper on plant manager best practices, the sponsoring vendor provides an easy way for readers to explore their technology via a recorded demo.

meridium   10 Mistakes Every Plant Manager Makes
_____

9 – 10 points: *Platinum*
Wow! You're either kidding yourself or you've mastered the art of plant management. Well done, but we know just how much work it is to maintain performance. It's time to look for tools that can make your difficult job easier to maintain over time.

Make your job easier with Asset Answers. <u>Watch the demo</u> to find out how.

This is a page from a research-based eBook. Right within the document the reader has easy ways to try the sponsor's technology.

STAGE 3: EVALUATION OF OPTIONS

Finally, you get to start talking about your offer! The information you provide here will help buyers determine how your solution differentiates from similar alternatives. Keep in mind, however, as mentioned earlier, the buyer might not have ruled out alternative approaches yet, and content should not exclude benefits of your solution over other categories completely.

It's important that you not only talk about what you do, but talk about how it is different from your direct competition. Help your buyer evaluate vendors by offering comparison checklists, RFP templates and Total Cost of Ownership and Return on Investment calculators. But most important, help your buyer convince the rest of their organization that you are the best choice by building a Champion Kit.

Building a Champion Kit

I was exploring Boston with friends from out of town and we stopped by one of the best-known open-air marketplaces.

The gentleman that you see hanging upside down, on the next page, was working the crowd. What you can't tell from the picture is that he spent the better part of a half hour gathering a crowd before executing his stunt. It was windy and a bit chilly and he was competing with a host of local bars, shops and various other acts. And yet, about 200 people were gathered, waiting to see the big trick. When he was done, a line of willing "financial contributors" were putting money in his out-stretched hat. How did he do it? He started with a few champions.

He carefully selected people passing by to help set up his props. These people attracted others by showing their interest. This hanging-upside-down stuntman was the ultimate salesman—earning his keep by drawing in a crowd.

Thankfully, most of us don't have to suspend ourselves from a 20-foot pole in windy downtown Boston to capture the hearts and wallets of our prospective buyers. But we do share a lot in common with this artist. People can usually live without our product or service. Our buyers have many other distractions and priorities on a daily basis. As much as it hurts to admit, we are replaceable. In the case of the stuntman, there was hot chocolate and live jazz right around the corner calling my name.

Organizations are complex webs of process, rewards, accountability and people. If you want someone who works at one of these organizations to pick you over an alternative, you have to instill into them some of the passion you exude for your business. The best way to do this is to build a partnership with an influential advocate. Good salespeople do this every day. They build rapport with someone who gives them the inside track of purchasing needs. Someone who tells them the "secret" threshold of pricing to ensure a smooth order process. Someone who lobbies to buy your product or service. But just like our stuntman, if you stop building advocacy after exciting your champion, success will vary. You have to make it easy for your champion to incite the crowd—just as he made it easy for his helpers to draw a crowd by giving them something to do, and often something to say.

Our buyer champions are good at their job, but they are generally very bad at selling our products internally. That's our job, and that's why I developed the notion of a Champion Kit. Champion Kits are *not* your corporate website. They are *not* a literature library. They are a series of tools designed to make it easy for your champion to build a business case.

The Four Components of Your Champion Kit

Making your internal champion an advocate hero can be a tricky path. Below are some of the tactics I've learned from years of trial and error. The tools in your Champion Kit will vary depending on your offering and the buyer's likely journey, but these four core components should be included.

1. **Justification brief** — This is not a pricing proposal, although pricing may make an appearance. This is an overview of the problem challenging the target organization, and an outline of various approaches to addressing the problem. It should also include a recommendation for why your champion is advocating your solution as the best approach.

2. **Buyers guide** — It would be lovely if our buyers didn't consider alternatives, but it would also be unrealistic. Instead of living in a fantasy land, arm your champion with a template that gives them various approaches to consider. Think of it as a checklist.

3. **Value calculator** — Help your champion quantify the likely impact your solution will have on the business. This could be dollars earned, risk averted, time saved or any other quantifiable measure.

4. **Presentation template** — Make it easy for your advocate to present to their management team. Give them the content of this kit in ready-to-use slides they can personalize. Don't forget to keep the template *simple*, because you want them to apply their own corporate design so it showcases as their work.

Four Tips to Remember When Building Your Champion Kit

1. **Don't forget objectivity.** Being impartial is difficult when your job is to sell your stuff. But if you throw objectivity out the window, you lose credibility, and no one will use your tools to help facilitate their internal purchase process. You need to balance natural bias toward your approach with evidence your champion can use that truly points to your solution as solving their business pain.

2. **Personalization, not customization.** The first time I developed a Champion Kit I made it far too complicated. The goal was to produce a customized, organization-specific business case. It was a noble goal, but I lost sight of one truth: people are easily distracted. Too much of the material was customizable and almost no one

used the kit. Instead, I started to give users the ability to personalize information without requiring heavy customization. It may not be as snug a fit, but it's far more important that the tool be used.

3. **Measure appropriately.** If you measure the kit's success on how many new leads you generate, you are going to develop the wrong content. While components of the kit could be used for driving inbound activity, the focus should be on your target audience who want to build a business case for your offering. You've already convinced them you are the right solution—now help them convince the rest of the company. Focus measurement on increasing your deal win rate and improving predictability of the closing portion of your buying cycle.

4. **Don't forget about kit adoption.** You can't treat the Champion Kit like publishing a whitepaper or data sheet. Humans are creatures of habit. If you want to introduce a new routine you have to work hard to build muscle memory. I learned this lesson the hard way. It is not enough to involve salespeople in the creation of the kit components; you must train them on how to use the tool, teach them why, and then challenge them to give it a try. To ensure adoption for my clients, I run a one-hour workshop on building champions and how to use the tool. Over the next few weeks I look for reps who have found success and encourage them to share it with their peers. This is especially important in the first 60 days of kit rollout. Once they see success, you can expect a snowball effect as they use, and reuse, the tool.

Just like our stuntman, building a champion kit requires some up-front planning, but when adopted by your sales community, reselling partners who are an extension of your sales team, and prospective buyers, it can lead to measurable reward.

STAGE 4: NEGOTIATION/PURCHASE

The sales team is going to take the lead during this stage of the buying process, but that does not mean marketing doesn't play a critical role. From pricing promotions to proposal templates, marketing is a key participant in this stage of the journey. Sometimes simply thanking buyers for considering your tool is all it takes to differentiate yourself from the competition. I recommend deploying strategic pipeline acceleration programs to help sales close deals and improve conversions rates during this stage.

Pipeline Acceleration Programs

These programs are not lead generation. They are efforts focused exclusively at moving existing opportunities through the buying process faster or with a higher win rate (not generating new opportunities). As a result, this tends to be one of the most underserved parts of the buyer's journey, since marketers are often directed toward "lead generation" as their primary goal. With a little planning, these underutilized techniques can have a significant impact on short-term revenue attainment.

Below you'll note a series of programs that I have executed many times across a variety of different businesses. While the specifics vary, the spirit of the programs remain the same.

- Lost–no decision email nurture

  If you are like most organizations, your team loses to "no decision" more often than specific competitors. While you weren't able to build a business case when the deal was first being worked, the latent need that initiated the opportunity likely still exists since the contact didn't choose an alternative. In most CRM systems, those deals will be marked as "lost–no decision" or some similar descriptor. Often by reengaging with these opportunities from the past 24 months, you can rejuvenate an opportunity that had been considered closed.

  Two key things to keep in mind when you reach out. First, make sure you pull opportunities that are more than 90 days old. You don't want to waste the time of someone who recently told you they were not ready to buy. Second, when you reach out, acknowledge your previous relationship. Rather than send a generic message about your services, spotlight new capabilities they may want to consider that have been developed since they last interacted with the team.

- Executive thank-you program

  Everyone wants to feel appreciated and sometimes a simple thank-you message from your senior executives is an ideal way to do that. In this message don't try to sell, but rather offer your sincere appreciation for their consideration of your solution, acknowledge they have a hard choice and offer a way to be in touch if they need help making a decision (and be available when they do). Don't expect a lot of replies, but know you are leaving a good impression. We launched this at one organization and saw a 12% increase in win rate. You might not get that much of a lift, but it takes very few resources, so any benefit is worth the effort.

○ Outbound support call

Prospective customers talk to their salesperson all the time. While this is valuable, they also want to know what their experience will be after a deal is closed. It's an easy and highly appreciated gesture for someone on the customer support team to reach out and introduce themselves. Their goal is not to sell but rather to answer questions and let your buyer know who is on their side after they join your customer community. This is not likely scalable across every opportunity, but is an effective technique for your most critical deals.

○ On-site "virtual" references

For complex buying processes, references are very important, but if you are like most businesses your happiest customers are guarded with gold. While they are happy to advocate, you correctly protect their time and the number of inquiries they receive. A nice way to get economies of scale is to offer a virtual roundtable where your advocate brings prospects on a tour of their facility/offices and hosts an open Q&A. While there is no formal presentation, the type of dialogue is what one would get in a reference call, only this time it's open for multiple prospects to participate at once. Be sure to invite participants who are not direct competitors, so they feel comfortable asking questions in front of others.

○ Special promotions to create urgency

Buyers who like our offering don't always want to purchase on our timeframe. Though I'd like to pretend it only matters that they buy at all, the truth is, we all live by financial commitments and often quarterly quotas. We need some percentage of buyers to move forward on our time scale. Special promotions can give a little incentive to buy now, rather than in 60, 90, or 120 days. Keep in mind promotions should only be used for opportunities you feel you have a good chance of closing, otherwise you risk degrading your value with buyers who will come back to you at a later time.

When building special promotions keep in mind that a discount is not the only card you can play. You can offer event passes, bonus features, even extended payment terms.

Mini Case Study: Using Special Promotions to Hit Quarterly Goals

We used this approach with a technology client of mine. Their long-term pipeline was strong, but they were anticipating that they would fall short of their current quarter goals. We selected the next quarter's opportunities that we felt were fairly advanced and offered each buyer a free pass to a major industry trade show that year if they purchased before quarter close. In addition, if they purchased two weeks before quarter close, they also received a VIP pass to the company's big awards banquet. The company not only met its quarter goals, it secured several walking advocates at the largest show of the year.

The program worked because:

1. We targeted opportunities that were likely to close—they simply needed a reason to close on our time scale, not their own.

2. The offer was of significant financial value and offered the champion a personal value while adding value to the company, which would likely have sent this person the show anyway and now saved on the entry price.

3. We made sure not to hurt the integrity of our financials. We set minimum deal thresholds and calculated commission to the salesperson on the deal size, minus the incentive. This allowed it to be a shared risk for the salesperson and the business overall and it was used selectively in opportunities they felt they could influence.

STAGE 5: DELIVERY OF PROMISE

At this stage, it's time to show a little love. Once the purchase has been made, you have to deliver on customer expectations, and while customer support and fulfillment might take the lead, marketing again has an important role to play. Consider how you can delight customers instead of just meeting their needs.

Help customers navigate using your solution to its maximum potential and remind them how much you value their commitment. As brand advocates, marketers have a lot to offer the process.

○ Frequent communications — Let them know where their order is in the processing queue, provide an easy mechanism to speak with someone for an update, and be proactive about potential delays.

○ Welcome kits — Welcome your new buyer to your community and make it easy for them to communicate with their organization by providing a customizable announcement they can simply edit and forward along. Explain what your offer does, and how it will benefit the company.

- ○ "Party in a box" — For large opportunities that represent strategic investment by your customer, send them a celebration "party in a box." They worked hard to select you as their partner—help them celebrate the decision. The kit can comprise any number of items, but consider a catered lunch, company-branded gifts, a dessert bar, even balloons strewn around the office that will help spread the good news—and make your champion look like a rock star.

- ○ Help them use your offering — Most important, make sure your users can quickly take advantage of your product or service. Send them training materials, onboarding courses, tips and tricks, and friendly reminders about what comes next.

STAGE 6: ADVOCACY

Turning customers into advocates is a treasure trove of opportunity that's often overlooked while we as marketers focus on loyalty programs to drive upsell and cross-sell. By creating opportunities for advocacy, our customers can be our best evangelists. Instead of simply focusing your efforts on penetrating new markets and acquiring new customers, marketers must also consider how to build a strong network of advocates within their existing customer base.

In today's buying and selling landscape, the importance of advocacy cannot be overlooked. Happy customers speaking on behalf of a company are considered more trustworthy—and more impactful toward helping prospective buyers make a decision. A whopping 92% of consumers trust recommendations more than any other form of marketing.[24]

Advocacy campaigns incentivize existing customers to vocalize and share their passion about your solution with their peers.

You can encourage this advocacy by linking happy customers to product review sites, connecting on social channels and providing a stream of content they will find

---

24 http://www.forbes.com/sites/kimberlywhitler/2014/07/17/why-word-of-mouth-marketing-is-the-most-important-social-media/#61623d357a77

relevant and shareworthy. You may even want to set up a formal referral program where customers are rewarded for introducing you to potential buyers. (You can learn more about this in Chapter 15.) Consider advocates who seek recognition from their peers, and give them opportunities to speak at events or be featured in case studies. Rewarding them for their activity can include the standard gift cards, but granting access to exclusive product upgrades, content, or other creative perks could foster greater affinity toward your brand than a simple gift card.

The Ugly Truth (and How to Overcome It)

I have a confession. The structure I outlined throughout most of this chapter is a bit deceptive. It gives the illusion of a linear process where buyers move from one step to the next. This is mostly accurate—however, it doesn't reflect how buyers interact with vendors.

The Buyer's Journey Is Not Linear

First, buyers don't start their process with our businesses; they can pop in at any stage of their journey. In fact, if we're developing effective content strategies, they will be finding us at many points across their investigative efforts. In addition, the time between stages is highly varied and the stages can sometimes overlaps, since buyers have their own timelines and internal process driving their priorities.

This truth makes it all the more important that you map out the entire buying process so that wherever they are in their process, you can be there to help.

I like to use a simple spreadsheet to inventory the process. In the top section I outline all the questions your prospect is likely to want addressed in each stage. When writing questions be very specific and avoid focusing on your particular offering. Remember, buyers want to understand the problem, the market and all their options long before they dig deeply into your offering.

In the bottom section, list what assets are available. If you've built personas, you will want to do this segmented by persona; but if you haven't finished that research yet, you can find great value in doing this at a general level. Don't worry if you have gaps—that's exactly what this exercise is designed to identify.

We began this exercise in Chapter 9 about lead nurturing where we mapped out the questions your buyers may want to ask at each stage of their journey. Here we will map the content you have available to answer those questions and identify gaps that need to be addressed.

Stage	Stage 1 Trigger	Stage 2 Solution Discovery	Stage 3 Evaluation of Options	Stage 4 Negotiation	Stage 5 Delivery of Promise	Stage 6 Advocacy
What questions does your buyer need addressed?						
List all assets available that map to this stage						

Content is not enough. You must create *trusted* content.

The difference between content and trusted content is not necessarily logical. There's some emotion at play when making any purchase, including complex B2B sales. Remember, your goal is to provide information, but simultaneously earn the trust of your audience. It takes being human to do that. People trust and buy from people, not faceless, anonymous businesses. Great content illuminates the personality and the people behind your content.

- List a real author for your eBooks and whitepapers
- Use video blogs to bring training and best practices advice to life—and use real staff, don't hire actors. Authenticity is obvious.
- Add your picture to your outbound emails
- Showcase employees on your website
- Sign every email with a real person's name
- Consider video chat technologies for online sales and support engagements
- Send personalized video introductions to bring your brand to life
- Integrate the advocacy of real customers whenever possible to validate your claims and prove support by a trusted third-party peer

CASE STUDY: MAPPING THE EXPANSION INTO NEW MARKETS

This analytics company sold software and services to a focused market segment—hospitality businesses. For years they had been very successful with this audience, living and breathing their needs, challenges, expectations and habits. The company had grown, was profitable and earned brand leadership in this niche market. They had a vision to accelerate growth by expanding into new markets where their specialized analytics would be attractive.

The Challenge

In making this leap they would be competing with large, established vendors that had strong technology mindshare. They not only needed to pivot the company brand to support a totally different buyer community—they needed to differentiate from the speeds and feeds that their competitors sold.

To start this journey, we mapped the buyer's journey for their known market to identify the base of content with which they could work. Initially, they thought it would be easy to "reverticalize" their existing content for another market segment, but two problems arose.

One, there were gaps in content for their core industry that they would need to fill for a market for which their awareness was close to zero.

And two, even more critically, reorienting content for a new market was not a trivial exercise.

The Thought Process

There were three choices for them to consider:

1. Find and replace industry terminology
2. Generalize existing materials so as not to be segment specific
3. Invest in new assets for the target market

Approach	Pros	Cons
Search existing assets and "find and replace" industry terminology	Quick to implement, costs very little to make the transition.	Not able to demonstrate a deep understanding of the new markets—a differentiator that had helped them stave off fierce competition in the niche market they currently served.
Generalize existing materials so as not to be segment specific	Once completed, it made creating new assets less resource intensive since multiple tracks were not required.	Risked alienating their current customer base with least-common-denominator value propositions and the illusion they were shifting focus away from the niche industry.
Invest in new assets for the target market	Most likely to resonate with the existing and future market. Demonstrates deep knowledge of buyer's pains and opportunities.	Time-consuming and resource-intensive.

They threw out the "find and replace" methodology, and began the process of expanding content into their new target communities.

What they found was a bit daunting. After mapping out everything they would need to go after this new market, they realized the task was a large one. Although they decided to move forward, the timeframe they had originally planned was unrealistic.

The Solution

They built a plan to sustain and grow, developing the content over time without disrupting business. This was both productive and protected their brand. They continued to win industry awards in their core market, protecting their market share while in parallel gaining early adopters in their new markets. With the help of these early adopters, the company was able to fill in some of these content gaps, secure in the knowledge they understood how their solution was applied.

It may not have been as easy as they expected, but in the end it was well worth the effort to develop a journey map, identify gaps, make a thoughtful decision, and thereby mitigate the risks of expansion.

HOW-TO GUIDELINES: MAP YOUR BUYER'S JOURNEY

Now you're ready to get to work and map your own buyer's journey. In summary, here is the process I recommend following:

1. **Conduct buying process persona interviews** and carefully map out how optimal buying processes are executed within the organization. Be sure to point out personality preferences by persona so the sales team can modify their approach as needed. (See Chapter 10 for questions to ask during the interviews.)

2. **Conduct buyer insight surveys across your various buyer types** (e.g., financial buyer, influencer and user community) to understand what actually initiates the need/desire for your offering. Be sure to take the participant back to the time before they started searching for a specific solution. You should try to identify 3–5 primary triggers.

3. **Inventory all your assets** and identify gaps you need to address by stage of the buying process.

Stage	Persona	Stage 1 Trigger	Stage 2 Solution Discovery	Stage 3 Evaluation of Options	Stage 4 Negotiation	Stage 5 Delivery of Promise	Stage 6 Advocacy
What questions does your buyer need addressed?	A	Q1 Q2					
	B						
	C						
List all assets available that map to this stage	A						
	B						
	C						

Note: I find it helpful to create the journey for each persona involved in the buying journey. And to color-code the asset boxes.

Green = Well covered

Yellow = Some coverage but additional assets required

Red = At risk—needs immediate attention

Using this system I can quickly look at this chart and know where my attention should be focused. This also allows me to have an easy dialogue with the balance of the organization to get their alignment behind my objectives.

4. **Create content that compares and contrasts various approaches** to help educate your buyer on which path would be best suited for their needs. Content starters might include:

   ○ "10 signs It's time to…"

   ○ "Three ways to…"

   ○ "Does your ____ pass the quality test?"

   ○ "Quantifying the value of ____"

   ○ "Eight ways you're doing ____ wrong"

   The key here is to focus on addressing the trigger relevant to your buyer and the various categories of solutions, not your specific offer.

5. **Arm your sales team with objective proof points and evaluation tools.** Checklists, evaluation guides and customer testimonials are helpful, but equally important is how you train your sales team to share the information. Help them take on the role of coach rather than just closer.

6. **Audit all your post-purchase communications** and look for opportunities to surprise customers by personalizing your communication tone, keeping them abreast of the status of their order, and generally reminding them they are just as important now as when they were negotiating an agreement. You'd be surprised how much of an impact changing little things like your on-hold message, or adding a personalized note on an invoices, can make.

   One place I've found the personal touch particularly valuable is when face time is in short supply. For example, when I run online workshops I often mail snack packs in advance to the client site where groups will be together to participate in the session. While I can't be with them in person, they can enjoy a little personal touch.

CHAPTER 12

Data, Meet Human

○ 57% of marketers say improving data quality is their most challenging obstacle.[25]

○ Only 37% of CMOs feel they are capable of using analytics to tailor their communications to consumers.[26]

I'll admit it: I'm a data junkie. I could spend most of my day playing with spreadsheets. Trend lines, bubble charts and bar graphs can make, or break, my entire day. Every once in a while I get completely lost in all the possibilities data provides. Yet, throughout my work with clients, I have been reminded that data itself is an amazing facilitator, but one that has limited capacity on its own.

Advances in technology are bombarding sales and marketing teams with growing volumes of data. With very little effort, marketers can see what our web audience has clicked on, the path they visited on our websites, how many emails were opened, and which ads are gaining attention. For even small campaigns this can lead to thousands, or tens of thousands of new data points in a single day. When it comes to large brands, the number of data points collected can amount to millions.

25 Informatica http://www.dnb.com/perspectives/marketing-sales/value-data-quality-marketing-success.html

26 A survey of over 300 marketing, IT, finance and management executives in the US https://www.marketingweek.com/2015/06/12/marketers-struggling-to-use-data-despite-stressing-the-importance-of-insight/

Consider a typical week of marketing for even a small organization:

Activity	Measurement Points
250 unique website visitors	Bounce rate # of unique visitors What pages were visited What assets were consumed What forms were completed Their navigation path Where they visited from (ad, search, referring site, etc.) The search terms that lead them to us Time spent on the site
3500 emails delivered	# of email opens # of click-throughs to embedded links # of forms completed/assets consumed # of unsubscribers # of bouncebacks
200 phone conversations	Who spoke to them What we learned on the call What assets we sent to them What questions they asked Whether a follow-up was scheduled
50 web seminar attendees	Who registered Who attended What questions they asked What drove them to register (website banner, email invite, telemarketing, etc.) How long they stayed on the session Whether they shared the recording

This relatively small week of activity added up to thousands of data points available for a marketer to review and act on. Now imagine what happens to these numbers when this brand's activity grows 10x or 100x or 1000x!

In today's technology landscape, the growing variety and adoption of marketing tools has made collecting these touchpoints an automated practice. That's an exciting prospect for the evolution of our space, but it has created a dangerous practice for marketers who may become dependent on this automation.

As part of this influx of information, data management has emerged as a kind of Achilles' heel for many companies. In some cases, as much as 55% of the data in our organizations is of poor quality according to a 2016 B2B Marketing Data Report by Dun and Bradstreet. This includes a variety of factors such as undeliverable email addresses, incorrect phone numbers, even missing firmographic basics such as company size and industry.

This chapter will review the manual checks and balances that are required to optimize machine processing of data for better conversion results.

FOUR WAYS THAT YOUR DATA IS LYING TO YOU

Because data is such a critical element of your marketing strategy, I offer a couple of simple rules of thumb: First, never take it for granted. Second, never take it in isolation. I like my data with a healthy dose of gut instinct and loads of qualitative information. When these are absent, I've found four very common ways that data is misunderstood and misused.

#1 Data tells us *what* but not *why*.

Data can provide incredible insights. When used properly it tells us exactly what an individual's journey has been. With proper tracking in place, we can see what a buyer read, which pages they visited, how long they watched certain videos, and even with whom they've spoken at the organization. But this behavioral data does not tell the underlying reasons behind their actions. To truly understand our customers, marketers must complement quantitative analysis with qualitative research to uncover our buyers' motivation. We must ask why.

#2 You risk losing the individual.

Understanding patterns allows our organizations to scale. We optimize communications based on A/B testing. We segment our database on profile data. We trigger campaigns based on recent event participation. All of this is valuable, except when it becomes the de facto driver of our strategy. When everything we do groups people together, we lose sight of the individual. One-to-one marketing might not be practical for most of us, but we should never give up the quest to integrate the individual into everything we do, even when using segmented marketing strategies. This means personalizing campaign communications based on persona insights, getting rid of fake send names, and reacting to the last action taken by the person. And most critically, understanding the whole person when making follow-up phone outreach.

#3 False confidence in the "funnel."

If you've read any number of marketing books or blogs, you've been introduced to (and likely inundated by) the concept of the lead funnel. This model dictates that marketers must build programs to focus on top, middle or bottom of the prospect funnel. This thinking has become the standard in the industry. We report on it. We segment based on it. We even customize our content for it.

But in reality, the funnel is not an accurate depiction of how our buyers engage with us, though the data in our systems may seem to convince us that buyers move linearly through our assets. In fact, it only looks that way because that is how we have set up and driven our campaigns. Buyers are on a journey that doesn't fit nicely into this outdated model. We will attract and engage people who are at different points in their journey, and this journey is not always identical.

It's our job as marketers to make relevant information about our brands accessible. By restricting content for specific "funnel" stages, we risk limiting its potential audience. Our job is not to segment out people from our content, but rather to attract people to it. In an era when buyers are researching the answers to their problems at their convenience, we had better give them what they need whenever they need it.

#4 Bad data leads to wrong conclusions.

Incomplete and inaccurate data can lead us to conclude that programs don't work, that our messaging is wrong, or that we are in a better position to meet goals than might be realistic. For example, a large manufacturing organization I worked with had tens of thousands of subscribers in their marketing email database. At first blush, it would appear that their entire target market was represented, and yet they knew of opportunities happening where they were left out of the short list of vendors to be considered, despite market leadership.

After digging deeper it turned out that two factors were contributing to a false sense of database completeness. First, their opt-out rate was shocking, with more than 40% of the database unsubscribed. Second, and likely what contributed to such a high unsubscribe rate, was the contact segmentation model in place. Based almost exclusively on website behavior, contacts were assigned attributes that indicated their function, industry and relevant products. These attributes were overlapping, inconsistent and never validated. As a result, individuals were assumed to care about a lot of things that were in fact not relevant to them. This misleading combination caused the company to make a lot of poor decisions before the truth in the data was revealed.

The Basics of a Data Intervention

When was the last time you did a manual quality check of your marketing data? If you're like most organizations, it was probably months ago at best, or, at worst, you've never actually reviewed your data. I hope you are sitting down because what I'm about to say might make you lightheaded. On top of everything else you already have on your to-do list, a routine manual marketing data check is an absolute must. It might be time to stage a marketing data intervention.

Before you stop reading in fear, let me tell you what's possible with some attentive marketing maintenance. By implementing manual spot checks you'll gain:

Loyalty from your sales team — Good-quality data takes away some of the excuses for ignoring leads, such as "the phone numbers were all wrong!" When salespeople can efficiently follow up, you've made them more productive, which is a surefire way to earn their trust. They'll not only fall in love with your leads, they love marketing just that much more.

Better email open rates — Aren't you tired of looking at low campaign open rates? It becomes very frustrating when your good content goes unread. Cleaning your database by validating email addresses and ensuring complete records allows you to not only properly segment your data, more important, it ensures that there are real, interested people on the other end of your efforts.

Higher conversion rates — Improving your data is the foundation of improving your conversion rates. When you are able to target more effectively, you'll see immediate improvements in everything from open rates to click-through rates to lead-to-opportunity conversions. According to research from the Aberdeen Group those who have good data quality spend 33% less time looking for data. That's 33% more time spent *acting* on data.[27]

Savings and investment clarity — In sales, time is money. In marketing, data is money. With poor data, you're wasting what's already a limited budget and resources that are already stretched thin. With more accurate reporting data, you can see what's really working across the business and what's contributing to revenue, allowing you to make better investment choices.

Opportunities to fine-tune automation — The need for manual checks will never go away, but you are likely to find patterns that you can build into your automation processes. For example, if you notice a spike in fake phone numbers, you can implement a phone number verification check. Or perhaps you note that many leads are getting through to the sales team from companies that fall below your target threshold. Perhaps augmenting your database with revenue data from a third-party provider would be a good step toward segmenting these companies out. The specifics you might find are endless, but you won't find them and improve over time without looking.

Our databases need care, attention and a whole lot of marketing love or we'll miss the opportunity to delight our buyers. This may seem obvious, so why are so many companies working with lackluster databases? Because maintaining good-quality databases is time-consuming, tedious work that happens behind the scenes when nobody is watching. What's more, those most qualified to roll up their sleeves and do it often find the task boring. Yet sometimes boring is exactly what we need.

CASE STUDY: THE TRUTH WITHIN THE DATA

There are few things in marketing that can make an almost immediate and huge impact on direct marketing success. Cleaning your database is one of them. There are hidden treasures in your database lost behind bad email addresses, faulty phone numbers and misunderstood interests.

---

[27] Aberdeen Research Report 2013 "It All Begins with Data Quality: Building the Foundation for Business Intelligence"

That's exactly what a newly expanded technology company uncovered. This organization was started in Europe and experienced healthy growth. Eager to capitalize on this momentum, they opened a U.S. office and tried many of the marketing and sales models that were born in their European offices.

The Situation

Though they brought on board some brand-name customers, the business was not growing at the pace they had hoped. After toying with lots of different approaches, the company knew it had to make a change. The product was solid and had been validated by their early customers, but sales growth in the U.S. had stalled.

The company's go-to-market efforts had been chasing anyone who would listen to their value proposition, and as a result their database had grown. The team felt confident the database was sufficient to meet their goals. In our early conversations about updating their marketing strategy, they told me they had 16,000 contacts in their marketing database. For a company that only wanted to close 10–20 strategic deals that year that number did seem sufficient. But based on their average weekly appointment rate and how many new deals were being entered into the pipeline, I realized we were either going to have to grow the database by 4X or dramatically change conversion rates.

The Problem

Their data was lying—a lot. A little due diligence proved important to developing our next steps. As it turned out, the perceived database size of about 16,000 contacts included more than 3,000 without email addresses. We were now down to 11,000 addressable contacts for our email marketing programs.

I then broke out the contacts by industry, since the company focused on just three vertical markets. Of those 11,000 with email addresses, about 1,000 fell outside of the target verticals, and over 650 records had no industry associated with them. This left us with 9,300 usable records. Of these, about 30% were irrelevant titles that they could not serve, and another 1% fell outside the geography they served. Then we discarded those contacts who unsubscribed from the database, and another 1–2% that were obvious junk email addresses (such as junk@gmail.com and student@yahoo.com).

At the end of this cleanup, less than half of the database we started out with was usable for targeted marketing programs. To that date, the company had been wasting more than half of its efforts marketing to irrelevant prospects.

The Cleanup

The numbers were scary, but now we knew where to start to build the database appropriately. We took a few steps to focus our cleanup efforts using company and contact-level information.

First, I looked up each and every one of the more than 650 company names that had no industry associated with them and tagged them with an industry code. By doing this, we uncovered another 350 companies in their target markets. Second, we deleted the obvious junk. Why clutter the database with data that is undoubtedly incorrect?

Third, we added a new field to the database called "function" and mapped every title (manually) to one of 7 standard titles, including "other." We use "other" to keep the data clean and not force a mismatched function. This allowed us to flag "other" records for more careful inspection. Any contacts that fell outside the targeted functions were irrelevant to our marketing and sales efforts, so they were archived out of the database for the purposes of outreach. With this in place, we could segment the audience by relevant responsibilities for well-targeted messaging.

Fourth, we pulled a rough company count using a free search tool, Hoovers List Builder, to assess how many companies were in the company's target universe. We selected the appropriate geography, company size and industry. This process revealed another 5,000 target companies for which we didn't have any contacts.

Fifth, we used an existing contact data provider to pull 712 names from these target companies who fit our target profiles to close that gap.

Sixth, there were a number of contacts in the target industry for which we did not have an email address. We used a combination of manual outbound calling and access to a subscribed database to append a verified email address to these records.

Last, we implemented new data policies that ensured that future focus would be on collecting contacts in the defined target industry within appropriate functions.

The results

In the end, the marketable database was smaller in quantity than the 16,000 they originally believed to have, but we were able to improve the quality of contacts that remained. This quality allowed us then to plan forthcoming marketing programs with confidence. The company was now ready to address the right contacts at the right companies, and maintain that data management plan on an ongoing basis.

HOW-TO GUIDELINES: DATA CLEANING COMMANDMENTS

Automation and data quality tools have dramatically improved database integrity, but they can't apply human intuition. The manual processes below are worth following to optimize your data quality, even when good automation processes are in place.

To put your best foot forward, commit to the following:

I shall regularly delete junk. Say it with me, "It's OK to delete data." No one likes to take names out of the database, but if a contact hasn't responded to a single piece of content in the last two years, or the phone number is disconnected, it's time to take a deep breath and let go! Take out those records with a name like Mickey Mouse and Joe Smith who work at ACME company. I promise—they aren't real people with real interest, or they would have given you a real name and address. Whatever criteria you build, just do it. Your response rates will go up, your measurements will be more accurate, and your energy can be focused on the prospects with true interest.

I shall partner with the rest of the company to fill in the blanks. It's great that someone visited the website and downloaded a few case studies. But what does the sales rep in the territory know about them? Do you know their physical location? Can you identify their industry? How large is their company? We create fields in our database for a reason—because they help us segment and align messages to buyer need. Don't let them sit empty.

I shall assess data quality on a quarterly basis. Sadly, most organizations do a one-time data-quality initiative where everything is in top order, and they feel great. Then, each week, each quarter, the quality slowly but continually degrades as prospects change jobs, new data flows in, and salespeople make more phone calls. Data quality *cannot* be a one-time, or even just an annual, process. Marketers should be reporting on it monthly, and commit to at least quarterly assessments and corrective steps. Use the same techniques you did for ad hoc list reviews—only this time, look across your entire database. You'll be shocked to learn how much your database has degraded over time. But with early and regular intervention you can stop the degradation from corrupting your marketing efforts.

I shall clean data before uploading it to the database. Before uploading a list into your database—for example, the attendee list from a recent trade show or webinar event—give it a manual once-over.

Look for the following:

- ❍ Are the columns labeled correctly? You'll be surprised how often data ends up in the wrong field because no one noticed incorrect labels.

- ❍ Find someone you know on the list. Does their data match what you know to be true? Or did rows become transposed by mistake?

- ❍ What fake names can you spot right away?

- ❍ Select a random handful of records and look up the person and company in LinkedIn, Hoovers or a data subscribed service. Does the data match?

I shall scan my new leads queue once a week. One low-tech but high-impact strategy to get ahead of data issues is to manually check the leads you're passing to sales. Look for leads sent that have not yet converted. Can you tell by looking at them that the data is poor of quality? Are you seeing the same name appear eight times in a row? Is there a bogus phone number? 123-555-1212 is not a real number. How many irrelevant titles are you seeing? Nothing is more effective than the eagle eye of a conscientious data-minded marketer.

I shall trust my common sense. We touched on this same advice in the chapter on lead scoring. It's worth repeating in the context of data management. In a world of automation, don't forget your strongest asset—your common sense. Do you think Jon Smith from ABC Company in Denver is the same person as Johnny Smith from ABC Company in Colorado? I bet it's the same person. You have common sense—it's OK to rely on it. Go ahead, merge the records!

I shall honor preferences and learn from unsubscribes. Don't force unsubscribes by giving contacts only one choice—get our email on our terms or don't get any at all. Provide them with the ability to limit topics of interest or frequency of communication.

Give them choices and honor their requests. Legalities aside, this is the right thing to do. If they do decide to leave, ask them why. A good percentage of people are willing to click a one-question survey to tell you why they are leaving. Try asking the following:

- Was the frequency of our communications too much?
- Did we bore you?
- Were we too impersonal?
- Was our message irrelevant?

Look for patterns that you can use to create better content, adjust to a more appropriate frequency and find the right tone of voice.

I shall ask relevant questions on registration forms. There is a limited number of fields a prospect will fill out before they abandon the form, so use them wisely. Avoid asking for data you can find by implementing data augmentation practices to find industry, company size and other easily attained firmographic information. When you do create a registration form don't be tempted to fill it with lead-routing questions. For example, aside from sending the lead to the appropriate sales territory, is it really important that the prospect tell you in what state they work? You can append this information later, and instead, focus on asking questions that are going to align messaging and future communications.

I shall build a complete profile of firmographic, demographic and psychographic data points. Firmographic, demographic, psychographic—oh my! What do all these terms really mean?

- **Firmographic data** refers to information about the company where your contact works—for example, its industry, number of employees, and headquarter location.
- **Demographic information** is basic profile information about the person, such as their age, education level, job title, job function and annual income.
- **Psychographic information** is behavior-based data on an individual. These are attributes that persona research helps you capture, such as how they make decisions, their aversion to risk, how transparent they are in communications and more.

Combined, these are the data types in a marketer's toolkit that allow us to be highly targeted, relevant, and effective—when we put a priority on data.

CHAPTER 13

This Is a Content Marketing Intervention

I only realized how serious my addiction was when, one day, my husband walked into my home office, took one look at me, and laughed. I had fallen deep into a spreadsheet rabbit hole while reviewing the results of a content marketing study. My hair was sticking up, three empty iced tea bottles were littered next to me and I had been staring so intensely at my computer screen, my eyes were squinting. My husband immediately staged an intervention.

"Hello, my name is Samantha, and I am a content marketing junkie."

I'm not the only one. Many organizations need a content intervention.

I'll admit, I've read business books on content. I follow content gurus on Twitter, for fun; I *enjoy* digging through survey responses on the topic; and I'm lucky enough to experiment with content for my clients every day. I'm addicted, and so are many of my peers.

We all know deep down that there is inherent value in creating and publishing content that illuminate the topics related to our products and services, the challenges facing our buyers, and the intersection of the two. However, though so many of us know content marketing is essential, many have yet to realize its true potential. Perhaps this is because content marketing is an inherent change to the way we've done our jobs in the past and there have not been many models for scaling efficiently.

- According to a TrackMaven report that looked at millions of communications from major brands, the output of content per brand surged 35% while its engagement decreased by 17%.[28]

- In fact, the gap is getting worse. As a whole, we're less effective now than we were last year. According to the 2016 Content Marketing Benchmark, overall content marketing effectiveness **dropped 8% from 2015 to 2016**.[29]

- The biggest issue plaguing our industry, however, is worse than ineffective content. There is an epidemic of wasting good content. According to SiriusDecisions, more than 60% of B2B content is never used.[30]

These poor results are pervasive because most content marketing programs are immature in how they scale content development, not because content marketing doesn't work.

In the early days of a content marketing program, making progress was relatively easy. When no formal content marketing is in place, everything we do makes a difference. But often, the ad hoc processes we build and our focus on "getting it done" actually hold us back from achieving our full potential.

Let's start by looking at the content creation process most companies follow. It is full of manual busywork that mires us in unnecessary steps. Here's how it works today:

- We start by assigning an author. That's assuming we have a subject matter expert on hand, or at least a coworker whose arm we can twist.

- To notify the author we send an email with the due date, topic and any guidelines we need them to follow, such as target word count and persona we're targeting.

- Then we send a friendly reminder via email as the due date approaches, just in case they got distracted.

28 http://marketingland.com/content-marketing-output-surged-35-in-2015-while-engagement-dropped-17-report-163979

29 http://contentmarketinginstitute.com/wp-content/uploads/2015/09/2016_B2B_Report_Final.pdf

30 http://www.fiercecmo.com/story/siriusdecisions-2014-more-60-b2b-content-ends-content-wasteland/2014-05-22

○ Uh-oh, much to our surprise (insert sarcastic tone here) we have to send a polite yet firm reminder email that our author has missed the deadline.

If you're wondering why we send so many emails it's because by now the writer is doing everything in their power to avoid eye contact with their editor.

○ Finally, we receive the draft copy.

○ Now we take the Word draft and move it to a shared drive for reviewers to edit.

○ Eventually the author sends you a note that all edits have been made and we confirm it's approved by the reviewers. Finally, it's ready for publication, so we copy the file to our publishing engine.

○ And if we're having a good day, we remember to send the author a link to the live post for them to share and bask in its published glory.

This process as described doesn't even take into account the design process, or eventual promotion of the content.

In this manual, ad hoc process, content strategists become little more than traffic police. Trust me, I know how hard this can be. As a certified type A personality I am drawn to my checklist because everything on the list seems important. But, while everything on the list may be important, it may not be valuable to our strategic goals. We need ways to distinguish what's really working from the busywork by cutting down manual processes that don't add value to the content creation process and focusing our efforts on up-front planning, customer insight and testing.

We have to stop this to-do list from taking over our days.

The fact that the above process is so common spurred me to conduct a content marketing survey to uncover where organizations can improve. A total of 132 marketers shared their biggest challenges, measurement priorities and content goals. Overall, the survey validated much of what ails the content-obsessed. But, more critically, it confirmed many of the best practices I have learned the hard way, through experimentation. (I may have eaten a few less pieces of stress chocolate if I'd known all this years ago!)

Tenets of Effective B2B Content Marketing

From my time in the content marketing trenches, and as illustrated by the findings of my survey of content marketers, I suggest anyone starting down the path toward content marketing nirvana follow these essential tenets.[31]

1. Lead by example

2. Experiment more

3. Document a strategy

4. Assign clear ownership

5. Collaborate more

6. Dedicate a budget

7. Don't forget a content promotion plan

8. Repurpose, repurpose, repurpose

Let's dive into each one of the eight tenets.

1. **Lead by example.** As leaders we have perhaps the most influential role in making content marketing successful. We need to lead by example. That means regularly contributing content for distribution. Whether it's a blog post, sharing existing assets socially, or simply participating in brainstorming sessions, showing our dedication is essential if we want the rest of the organization to follow.

2. **Experiment more.** Content experimentation rules the airwaves. In the benchmark study, those marketers whose content marketing underperformed had tried publishing far fewer content types than those who reported great success. Embrace the variety of our digital age. Some readers prefer short-form content others are highly visual learners. What's more, there are more ways than ever for your audience to find your content online, so the greater your variety of content formats, the greater your likelihood of avoiding that dreaded dilemma of content waste. Some formats to consider:

---

31 https://www.percussion.com/Assets/www.percussion.com/resources/whitepapers/CM-Benchmark.pdf

THIS IS A CONTENT MARKETING INTERVENTION

- ○ Infographic
- ○ Instructographics (how-to, steps)
- ○ Poster
- ○ Checklist
- ○ Quick guide (3–5 page)
- ○ Case study
- ○ Worksheets or templates
- ○ Tear sheet (or quick reference guide)
- ○ Expert Q&A podcast

- ○ Video interview
- ○ Slideshare
- ○ Interactive quiz
- ○ eBook
- ○ Whitepaper
- ○ Interactive quizzes
- ○ Email course/newsletter
- ○ Live webinar event
- ○ Podcast series
- ○ Research report

3. **Stop winging it, document a content strategy!** Having a documented content strategy is directly correlated to success. Multiple industry studies, including mine, have shown that this is a key contributing factor to the success of your content marketing efforts.

> When you are ready to get started I invite you to use the handy content strategy template   http://www.unleashpossible.com/templates.   It's structured as an Excel template with several sheets so you can go from thinking about writing a plan directly to action in digestible steps.

Your content marketing strategy should include components related to both planning and execution to provide direction and focus for your employees within a clear course of action. Consider including:

1. Mission statement
2. Content KPIs
3. Target audience
4. Content inventory
5. Buyer's journey
6. Master themes
7. Contributing authors
8. Targeted keywords
9. Distribution channels
10. Roles and responsibilities
11. Content SLA to eliminate review bottlenecks

In the How-To Guidelines later in this chapter I explain each component in greater detail.

4. **Assign clear ownership.** When assigning a Content Marketing Manager keep in mind that in addition to serving as writer, editor and community advocate, this individual also needs to play the roles of:

    Juggler — These professionals juggle deadlines, authors, whitepapers, blog posts, article and egos. I recently encountered a marketing content calendar with six different content formats and 63 deliverables all to be produced within 90 days.

    Brand ambassador — Great content marketers not only advocate for your brand in the content they produce, they are also the stewards of your brand standards across the company. It is the responsibility of this individual to ensure that all published pieces maintain the same brand representation by managing other authors and teaching them how to represent your brand and appeal to your buyers consistently.

    Chief Nag Officer — No one wants to admit to nagging their colleagues, but in a world full of distractions and competing priorities, the truth is, nothing crosses the finish line without a little coaxing. (As the most experienced content marketers know, in many cases it requires a *lot* of coaxing.)

    Analyst — It's not enough to do a lot of things, you need to do a lot of the *right* things. Select a Content Marketing Manager who is naturally driven by measurement and inquisitive enough to lead the effort in establishing content marketing metrics.

    After assigning this resource, resist the temptation to distract them from their core mission. Content Marketing Managers are strategic, and central to the performance of this core business capability—they are not solely writers. They should be focused on strategic content creation and promotion to market your company, not be pulled into everything that needs to be written.

5. **Content marketing is a team sport, collaborate more.** While it's important to have appropriate staffing and resources on hand to execute a content marketing strategy appropriately, the size of your marketing team has no correlation to success. This is due to one of the core credos of content marketing: it must represent the various strengths of your business entity. Marketing, therefore, does not have a monopoly on quality content.

What new ideas, subject matter expertise, and domain knowledge could you uncover if you tapped into the rest of your organization? Try to encourage at least 10% of your company to contribute to the content marketing effort. It doesn't matter what the job, the larger team has something of value they can contribute. For example, consider:

○ FAQs by your support team, who hear customer inquiries daily on the front lines of the business.

○ A day in the life of a purchasing agent

○ Tapping into sales to profile a customer per week

Don't forget—not all content has to come from within your organization. Your customers want to hear and see marketing that reflects their values and to which they can relate. Who better to serve as content creators, than your customers? All you have to do is *ask*!

For example, after a recent visit to the Museum of Science here in Boston I received a post-visit survey. It contained an incentive to enter to win free passes for completing the questionnaire. I was happy with our visit and rated everything well—except for our experience in the café, which was unfortunately more of a science experiment than an enjoyable meal. At the end of my survey, the thank-you page directed me to popular review sites where with one click I could post a review of my visit. I would never have taken the time to write a public review on my own, but the one-click prompt coaxed me to take the extra time. This action seems very natural in the B2C world, yet we hesitate to do it in B2B environments. It's time we moved beyond our hesitation. If no reputable review site exists for your category of offering. create your own review page. It's worth capturing good spirits when customers are fresh from interacting with your team.

Beyond survey responses and reviews, you can go one step further by asking customers to write guest blog posts, to be featured in an interview with short video comments, and more. Get creative about your request, because the worst they can say is "No, thanks."

Another source of external content bandwidth is professionals who offer specialized skills in producing content marketing assets. In the research study, 66% of those who exceeded expectations for their content marketing paid for third-party written content, compared to 21% of those rating themselves below expectations.[32] Not only should you consider hiring professional writers, but also influencers who bring both audience and expertise to complement your efforts.

6. **Dedicate a budget.** The most successful content marketing teams are lean, mean productivity machines, but that doesn't mean they operate without a budget. Dedicated budget should be allocated to the critical components of an effective strategy. When budgeting, plan for experimentation with content formats, paid distribution tactics to drive readership, and recruiting a variety of authors.

   When evaluating previous content marketing activity look with a discerning eye at the performance of various tactics. Seek to double down on the activities that are working well, and decrease budget in areas that did not help you meet your content marketing objectives. (Hint: if you operated last year without content marketing objectives, start there.)

7. **Don't forget a content promotion plan.** If you create it, they will <u>not</u> come! One of the biggest differences between content strategy and content *marketing* strategy is promotion. Without it, your content risks going unused and unseen. There are a number of ways to promote content using existing resources, the first of which is your email list of customers and prospects. When engaging with this community, segment your content as much as your database and bandwidth allow for regarding titles, industry, persona, etc. Many pieces of content you create can be slightly reworked to fit a different audience—for example, simply by updating keywords and the title of the piece. Doing so will increase the likelihood of a member of that audience opening your email and engaging with the piece.

   Your sales team is also an ideal channel for content promotion. Sending something of value such as a new eBook or piece of thought leadership is greatly preferred to the dreaded "just checking in" message to a target account they are working. What's more, engaging with existing customers using an occasional piece of well-written content marketing is a nice way of staying in touch outside of upsell or renewal conversations.

   If you're in need of expanding your universe of prospects and increasing eyeballs on content to generate net new leads, be sure to budget for paid content promotion

---

32 https://www.percussion.com/resources/content-marketing/white-papers/content-marketing-benchmarks-report/index.html

tactics. There are many syndication partners that will put your content in front of a targeted audience (for a fee). You can also partner with a public relations agency to secure highly targeted bylined articles and guest posts on industry trade sites, using that opportunity to link back to your gated piece of content. Many industry publications also allow for paid promotion to their email database, a perfect opportunity to promote your content and collect email addresses, all while providing something of value to their member community. Also consider tactics that eat up time, not necessarily budget. Partner with complementary organizations in your space to offer a partner webinar, cross-promoting to each others' databases. Conduct influencer outreach and feature thought leaders in your space in a resource. It's not time-consuming for them to respond to one question—and, of course, don't forget to ask them to share the final piece.

As with all marketing tactics, the rule of thumb in content promotion is to focus on the channels and tactics that resonate with your specific audience. Much can be revealed about the path forward when you consider referral sources to your website and blog, examine persona interviews, and research how specific groups in your customer community find new content.

8. **Repurpose, repurpose, repurpose.** Remember to reuse content in different formats whenever possible to minimize production costs and maximize exposure. One cornerstone piece of content, say a whitepaper or eBook, contains insights that can formulate, for example, a series of blog posts promoting the original piece, the subject of a Q&A video interview with a company executive, a guest byline article for a partner or industry publication, a live webinar event, an infographic, and many other formats. Publishing across multiple formats helps improve SEO results, and increases the exposure of your message across all the various formats your audience may be engaging.

Overall, content marketing is not just another name for demand generation—it is a fundamental shift in responding to the ways buyers purchase. It's not a fad. It is not a revolution. It's a natural evolution in the way we market and sell. The sooner we embrace its best practices, the more effectively we market.

CASE STUDY: BREAKING THE FEAR OF VIDEO

This software company had a mission to drive more blog traffic around their thought leadership platform.

Until that time, the organization had focused on traditional text-based blog and PDF assets. The company sold to marketers, a group that values creative and engaging content perhaps even more than other buying segments. We hypothesized that adding video to their mix would break from the tradition, catch the attention of our discerning audience, increase traffic and do so in a cost-effective way.

The Problem

My client had shied away from video in the past because of a fear of the unknown. They felt video would be hard to produce in the type of consistent cadence we needed without breaking the budget. I convinced them that a video interview series for the blog would be both attainable and practical, given their on-staff personalities and ability to pull together influencers in the space.

But, I'll be honest—when they asked me to host the series, my own fear crept in. I was hesitant. Though we were passionate about the topic, with a list of fantastic guests, I worried whether we would be able to provide consistency. I worried about having enough to wear. I even worried about hearing my own voice on film!

Seriously, these are the thoughts that went through my head. These are common fears that we can all relate to. Perhaps they have been what has kept you from a new content format in the past.

The Solution

Rather than trying to create a video production house in this software company, we treated video like an experiment. This mindset meant creating a hypothesis, moving quickly and, most important, measuring results.

We introduced two types of video segments: short videos of employees sharing insights and experiences, and interviews that hosted guest marketers talking about various topics related to content marketing. Using existing staff with video and editing capabilities, plus $400 of equipment, we built our own makeshift studio. We needed lights, a green screen, stands to hold an iPhone for sound capture, and a tripod for an existing camera. Once we set up our space, and experimented with this new format, we found that our fear of video was completely unwarranted. Not only did we produce great videos, we exceeded our expectations by producing quickly and consistently.

Idea Generation Coming up with video ideas was easier than we expected. We kicked off the series with a brainstorm session that led to our first two talks and a couple of interview candidates. As it turned out, inspiration was all around us, and after our first brainstorm, scheduling a weekly video taping session became an easy part of our cadence. To maximize our resources, we thought about how video could be applied to programs we were already executing. To keep the flow of interviews strong, we focused our efforts on finding individuals with a point of view rather than sticking rigidly to a script, though everything tied back in some way to the overarching theme related to the software. We quickly learned not to be afraid to ask for participation. Rarely did anyone say no—and when they did it was almost always accompanied by a referral to a peer.

Scheduling Being flexible with studio time turned out to be essential for capturing people when they could squeeze us in, so we made sure two people on the team knew how to capture the footage. We recruited well in advance of when we needed video, some weeks capturing two or three videos and others having no guests. This approach ensured that we always had a backlog of quality content to share without the stress of being beholden to a taping schedule.

Optimization This series was all about sharing ideas. We worked hard to put our participants at ease, encouraging a conversational tone and never subjecting them to more than a couple of takes. In response to the short attention span of viewers we added a second camera angle to accommodate our interview format—more eye contact increased the average video duration of our viewers. We also cut longer videos into shorter segments.

Promotion On average, each video was shared 65 times, driving the majority of our traffic (67%). During our experiment, the only active promotion we did was to tag the speaker on Twitter and send out an internal email making the team aware the video was posted. We believe additional focus on other channels, including LinkedIn and cross-promotion on landing pages, would have driven even further engagement.

The Results

Dipping our toe into video production was very rewarding and much easier than we had expected. In 90 days, our experiment achieved our mission and dispelled the myths that video was too hard.

Not only did we attract more visitors with this new format, we increased the engagement of these visitors on the site itself. The total number of blog views increased by 38.5%, and this influx of traffic increased readership of non-video content by 9.5%. We learned that viewers tuned in for an average of 1:24 minutes, then stayed on the blog for much longer, consuming other posts related to the topic. Win–win!

HOW-TO GUIDELINES: 11-STEP CONTENT MARKETING STRATEGY

When setting out to establish a content marketing strategy, consider these 11 key components:

1. Mission statement

Your 50-words-or-less content marketing mission will become your content mantra. Make it relevant to your business, make it inspirational and make it count! Your mission statement should include a description of your audience, how you make their lives better and what you will deliver for them.

For example, my blog's missing statement is this: "To inspire marketers and entrepreneurial leaders to unleash the possible within their organizations by providing practical advice for improving sales and marketing collaboration that results in business growth."

2. Content KPIs

Content KPIs (key performance indicators) should measure a wide spectrum of performance across productivity, awareness and demand acceleration. If you have a broad range of content themes and personas, it will be helpful to measure KPIs by content theme, format and persona. Eventually you'll even want to evaluate KPIs by author or distribution channel. You may even want to prioritize one part of the business over another to align to revenue goals. But whatever you choose, don't bite off more than you can chew. Start by monitoring aggregate statistics for the most pressing part of your business, until you can acquire a content analytics system that facilitates detailed segmentation.

3. Target audience

Great content marketing isn't about your brand—it's about your audience. It's tempting to presume we understand enough about our audience because we are familiar with how they interact with our business. But this assumption is a gross oversimplification of the truth. You not only need to understand what content is valuable to them in connection with your brand, but what content they value beyond what pertains to your products and organization. Find out what problems they're looking to you to solve, and what questions they have along the way. Get a sense for the appropriate tone and formats that will be most helpful to your target reader(s), and the path toward content marketing success will grow increasingly more clear.

4. Content inventory

Unless you have been operating in total isolation, you already have content that you can use in your content marketing efforts. These can be assets you've created or material you curate from other sources. It's important to create an inventory of all those assets so you can map them against the buyer's journey you will outline. Even if you have an asset that doesn't quite meet your current standards or is outdated, note it in the inventory process. With some clever editing you may be able to update the content within a particular segment or alter it to suit that segment. Identify high-priority gaps and use that to create your 60-day editorial calendar.

5. Buyer's journey

As more buyers self-educate and conduct research online (often without talking to anyone from your sales organization), your content must stand as a proxy for parts of the sales process. Throughout their journey, they'll have specific questions and needs. Once they do interact with sales, your efforts in lead nurturing rely on well-planned content to keep buyers engaged, with appropriate messaging for their given stage in the journey.

A well-planned content map will ensure that you have sufficient content aligned to each stage of this buyer's journey. To build a solid content map, start by identifying key questions and data points your audience will value at each stage of the path. If you have buyer personas, a good rule of thumb is to aim for 3–5 content assets per persona per stage as a starting point. Make sure to identify the asset title and format(s), and use this map to determine which content elements need to be produced first. Remember to reuse content in different formats whenever possible to minimize production costs.

Awareness Building	In this early stage you want to stay away from content about your offering. Focus instead on benchmark research, survey reports, trend studies and industry news.
Problem Identification	In this phase your buyer is starting to identify areas of opportunity within their own organization to improve. Content such as self-assessments, case studies and checklists are particularly valuable.
Evaluating Solutions	Unless you have a monopoly (and who does anymore), there is likely more than one solution to the problem that your offer solves, including the option to do nothing or build a custom solution. Content here should help buyers understand why inertia is the wrong approach and identify the unique ways working with a third party benefits them. Be careful to focus on approach validation vs. your specific offering.
Vendor Selection	Buyer's guides, competitive comparisons, and product reviews are essential elements to any vendor selection content plan. You will also want to heavily emphasize your approach to service, spotlight customer satisfaction and highlight staff thought leaders and third-party influencers who validate your approach.
Negotiating	ROI calculators, justification briefs, proposal templates, executive outreach, promotions and TCO case studies are very relevant for this stage of the buyer's journey.
Implementation	Enabling buyers to successfully leverage your offer is the most critical component to building references and an ongoing revenue stream. Implementation-stage content should include how-to videos, user stories, FAQs and documentation.
Advocacy	A content strategy's job is not done once a buyer becomes a customer, but many content marketers stop prior to this stage. Instead, map specific content plans that focus on renewal revenue streams and creating brand advocates and ongoing loyalty. This can include something as simple as holiday greetings or emergency response communications or training on new capability launches.

6. Master themes

It's relatively easy to write about our offerings, but it's rather difficult to write about our buyer's challenges. Many editorial calendars are structured around only product-related launches and features. Consider not only what problems your buyers face day-to-day, but also what larger themes are current within the industry. By developing a series of master themes, you can provide a framework for developing content that will resonate with your audience, inspire your writers and provide consistency of messaging through keyword usage, tone, etc.

7. Contributing authors

The best way to generate large volumes of high-quality content is to enlist the help of subject matter experts in your organization, or externally. Consider the topics valuable to your buyer personas and who in your company or industry possesses authority on these topics. A single writer might be able to support multiple personas, but the themes that inspire them will be different. Writers can come from many places—industry associations, consulting organizations, across your entire business, among your customer community, and more.

> Download the full workbook at http://unleashpossible.com/templates

8. Targeted keywords

Effectively using keywords ensures that your target audience discovers your content in their online searches. The key is to use those keywords in the appropriate context and to use them frequently. Old tactics of keyword stuffing to optimize the page for search engines no longer work, since Google and other providers update their algorithms, so it's important that your subject matter experts are prompted to use keywords in the appropriate context. Since frequency in context is important, you'll want to focus on a relatively short list of critical keywords that will have the most impact on SEO. The keywords you select can be a single word or short phrases.

9. Distribution channels

You've got a fantastic set of content assets ready to produce, but you've got to consider how to generate eyeballs on this great work. Don't forget to think about promotion. Where are you going to distribute your content for maximum conversion and engagement?

Content distribution channels:

- Social media (Twitter, LinkedIn, Facebook, Instagram, SnapChat)
- In-house email database
- Purchased or rented email database
- Via link on company blog post
- Via links on contributed article/guest blog posts
- Press releases
- Banner ads
- Paid content distribution networks

I recommend estimating the engagement you'll see from each channel (as part of your targeted KPIs, as discussed earlier). If your target KPIs don't map to your current audience, start playing with content frequency and the variety of content produced.

10. Roles and responsibilities

You've outlined some great opportunities to generate content that converts. You know what you want to measure. And you know the key topics you want to cover for the personas you want to focus on. Now, who is going to coordinate all this work? Whether your team is three people or 300, it's important to outline clear lines of responsibility. Use the following guide as a starting point.

Responsibility	Assigned to:
Maintain and publish editorial calendar	
Proofread content prior to publication. Does it vary by persona or content theme?	
Develop/maintain brand and tone of voice guidelines	
Master keeper of the keyword list	
Document content brainstorm sessions for future reference	
Produce weekly content KPI reports	
Train content contributors to use your content management system	
Design content approval workflow	
Alert writers to pending content deadlines	
Nag writers who have missed content deadlines (No one wants to be a Chief Nag Officer, but sometimes we have to prod to create urgency)	
Coordinate promotion across social channels	
Monitor keyword use in press releases	
Monitor keyword use in web copy	
Monitor keyword use in product collateral	
Train sales to leverage content assets during the sales process. Does this vary by persona or content theme?	
Survey audience for feedback on content assets being produced	
Review personas on a quarterly basis for shifts in need	
Maintain content inventory, including retiring or updating assets that are no longer relevant/timely	
Monitor competitor content production to assess relative share of voice and effectiveness	
Manage content creation budget	

11. Use content SLAs to eliminate review bottlenecks

Long ago, in a dark windowless office, I sat frustrated reviewing my team's content deliverables. We were responsible for a new market segment within a mature software business. The content review processes we were expected to follow were built to support a 20-year-old, billion-dollar business. Nothing about that suited our needs.

We had an aggressive content schedule, access to plenty of subject matter experts, and we knew what we were producing was resonating with our audience. The problem was that it took too much time and coaxing to move assets across the finish line. The more we produced, the worse the problem became.

We had to find a way to eliminate the bottlenecks in our content production process. After a failed attempt to simply ignore the big company process I inherited (being chastised for that didn't deter me, but the threat of reducing my budget changed my behavior), I found the solution in the form of documented content service-level agreements, or SLAs.

A content SLA is a written agreement between you and your content stakeholders that outlines policies, procedures and timelines that you both agree to follow. It sounds stiff and boring, but it works. Many years later I've found content SLAs a helpful foundation to forming, and keeping, shared goals across a wide variety of organizations, large and small.

Five Signs You Need a Content SLA

Not every team needs to document a content SLA, but some teams will benefit greatly from one. If you suffer from all or some of the symptoms below, it's time to consider an SLA intervention.

1. You consistently miss content delivery targets

2. More than 15% of your time is spent chasing down deliverables

3. Just when you thought an asset was ready to publish, last-minute edits derail your plans

4. You find yourself focusing on specific topics, not because your audience prefers them, but because it's easier to finish this type of material

5. Content authors and reviewers complain that everything they are asked to do is urgent and last-minute

What Your Content SLA Should Include

Content SLAs hold editorial staff, writers and reviewers accountable to delivery timelines that builds trust and consistency. Your documented content SLA should answer these important questions:

THIS IS A CONTENT MARKETING INTERVENTION

○ Who will review content?

○ How long will they have to review assets? Does it differ by topic or asset type?

○ How will you communicate deadlines?

○ How are edits to be submitted?

It may look something like this chart.

	Messaging Brief	First Draft Review	Second Draft Review	Review in Layout	Publish	Promote
REVIEW COMMITTEE						
Mandatory	Content Marketing Manager, Product Manager, Industry Evangelist (for thought leadership/issues pieces)	Content Marketing Manager, Product Manager, Industry Evangelist (for thought leadership/issues pieces)	Author content attributed to, PR Manager (if press release by-lined article), Content Marketing Manager, Product Manager, Industry Evangelist (for thought leadership/issues pieces, VP Marketing	Brand manager, Author content attributed to, Content Marketing Manager, Product Manager, Industry Evangelist (for thought leadership /issues pieces), VP Marketing	Content Marketing Manager	Campaign Manager, Social Media Manager
Optional	Sales Representative			Campaign Manager, Social Media Manager		
REVIEW TIMES						
Blog Post		2 Business Days	Not Applicable	Not Applicable		
Whitepaper		10 Business Days	5 Business Days	2 Business Days		
eBook		10 Business Days	5 Business Days	2 Business Days		
Infographic	Conference Call	5 Business Days	2 Business Days	5 Business Days		
By-lined Article	Messaging Brief	5 Business Days	2 Business Days	Not Applicable		
Presentation		10 Business Days	5 Business Days	2 Business Days		
Research Paper		10 Business Days	5 Business Days	2 Business Days		
Press Release		2 Business Days	2 Business Days	Not Applicable		
COMMUNICATION PROTOCOL						
Communications	Calendar Invite: CONTENT INPUT: Asset Description, Target Audience	EMAIL SUBJECT LINE: Content Review: Due Date DAY-MONTH Name of Asset	EMAIL SUBJECT LINE: 2nd Draft Review Due Date DAY-MONTH Name of Asset	EMAIL SUBJECT LINE: Design Review: Due Date DAY-MONTH Name of Asset		

How are edits/ questions to be submitted? In each review communication we will link to the asset that needs to be reviewed and provide instructions for inputting your suggestions. Generally content will be placed on a shared drive where you can add comments and edits directly to the document.

What happens if a reviewer does not respond? Our goal is to produce timely, high quality content that resonates with our audience. That requires consistency of a publishing schedule. As such, if you do not respond to a review cycle, we will assume your consent to proceed forward. If you are unable to meet a review SLA, you may assign someone to take your place, or contact us to make alternative arrangements. A partnership is based on trusting each other. Please trust us to keep the process moving forward, and we promise to raise red flags should content contain anything we know to be of concern to the organization. By building a predictable process we hope to avoid content review cycles falling therough the cracks,minimize last minute requests and have maximum participation without generating extra burden on your time.

How frequently is the editorial calendar updated? A link to the editorial calendar will be sent on a monthly basis. However a live link will be available to view the latest version. It can be found here (insert link). We welcome suggestions for new content and invite you to share ideas in our monthly brainstorm sessions. You may also send topic requests to (insert email address).

Editorial calendar reviews The first Monday every month we will hold an editorial calendar review meeting. To be added to the calendar invite please email (insert email address). If you are unable to attend you are welcome to send a proxy in your place. Ad hoc content requests are welcomed, but we encourage you to use the monthly session to maximize planning and avoid overlapping deadlines.

Helpful Tips

Content SLAs can be a very valuable tool when executed effectively. Follow these guidelines to make sure you make the most of yours.

Don't be a dictator — When you document SLAs it's easy to tell people what to do, but it won't work. Even if what you are asking is valid, it is likely participants will rebel against the process. Be sure to include key stakeholders in developing SLA terms.

Hold yourself accountable — Content SLAs should hold accountable not only authors and reviewers, but also the editorial process. Resist the temptation to treat every request with the same level of urgency, and formulate consistent review mechanisms and response processes.

Explain the "why" — For the best success, make sure your content team understands why the SLA is being created and what you hope to gain by implementing the process.

Leverage an executive sponsor — Nothing can derail a plan faster than a key contributor ignoring the process. It can create a cascading impact on the team as a whole. Enroll an executive sponsor (for example the CMO, VP Marketing, or Product Management Leader) to facilitate the rollout of the SLA.

Use your common sense — No documented plan is going to account for every conceivable scenario. Make sure you cover the most common scenarios and use common sense to fill in the gaps.

CHAPTER 14

Buzz – The Modern PR Imperative

By guest author Katie Martell

What do you want to be known for?

I don't mean your personal legacy, but rather, that of your business? Whenever I am asked about the definition or the purpose of public relations (PR) in the age of digital marketing, I reply with this simple question. Managing the perception of a brand doesn't happen by accident. Today we are inundated with between 500 and 3,000 (if not more) marketing messages every single day. It's never been more important to stand out in this clutter, break through this noise, and catch the attention of our customers.

But PR doesn't stop at attention. It is a continuous and very intentional strategic act of positioning your brand as a trusted resource in your industry, of raising the profile of your executives and brand stewards to a position of authority, and of earning air cover while your business does what it needs to do—grow. Great PR takes into account who matters in your space, and what they're talking about, and it works with timely precision to insert your brand message into that narrative.

As the marketing landscape evolves, so does this age-old tactic. Even the way we talk about it has evolved. When Samantha and I thought about the right title for this chapter, we realized "PR" in the traditional sense is not what companies need in their playbook. Our priority in marketing today is truly to create *buzz*, and to ensure that our brands are everywhere they need to be to influence customers to action. In a digital marketing world, creating buzz has become a highly orchestrated combination of tactics. Any tactic that exists in a silo doesn't work. Consider buzz building as the new intersection of thought leadership, content, SEO, social media, awards, speaking, influencer engagement, and events.

The next time someone asks you, "Should we invest in PR?" remind them: buyers don't do business with companies they've never heard of, and brands they do not trust.

A Note about Measuring Buzz

How do you measure the efforts to create buzz when the goals of these initiatives are so lofty and strategic? In a digital world where conversion rates are measured and optimized down to fractions of percentage points, how do you measure "raising brand awareness" and "managing brand perception" or "thought leadership"?

I learned from my time at a communications firm (Version 2.0 Communications) that the best approach to measurement is to be consistently reflective, rather than ad hoc. Like any other marketing initiative, setting objectives at the outset of a program or campaign is paramount. Three common mistakes are to set unrealistic goals (for many niche technology firms, *New York Times* coverage may simply not be possible), to measure too infrequently (many industries, especially technology, move at the speed of light, and programs should be calibrated appropriately), and to measure the wrong things.

Beyond the basics, such as impressions, social mentions, follower growth and amount of coverage, consider looking at:

- How frequently *key messages* are picked up and amplified
- How coverage compares to at least two competitors
- Top referring sites driving traffic back to your site
- Survey tools to benchmark whether your audience is aware of you
- Sources of new contacts in your marketing automation database (and if tied properly to revenue, this can indicate which referrers are driving real revenue)

You may know, deep down, that a strong buzz strategy is a necessary part of your overall marketing plan. Your instincts are not wrong, but in the data-driven world of business, you've got to be as good at *measuring* your results as you are at attaining them. Advocate for your buzz program with consistent measurement, reporting, and a little bit of internal PR.

CASE STUDY: CREATING BUZZ TO BUILD AWARENESS AND TRUST

Building brand awareness as a new market entrant is never an easy feat. The challenge becomes more difficult when your organization is up against industry giants, with large budgets and established market presence. It becomes increasingly implausible when the industry you're operating in is riddled with dishonest, unreliable players.

The Challenge

This early-stage B2B organization provided contact and business intelligence to businesses. As employee number 12, my primary task was to raise the profile of our new brand to compete among entrenched players with millions more in their budgets and strong existing brand awareness. We played the game as if we were David facing off every day against Goliath.

Not only did we compete with the big dogs, we operated within a highly commoditized market. If you've worked in business for a while, you've likely seen an unsolicited message from overseas vendors in your inbox offering "3M decision makers available with validated email and phone for use in your marketing and sales efforts." These scams were rampant, and the quality of their information was hugely problematic, but yet, this was part of our perceived competitive set.

Our buyers learned to delete these messages instantly, and ultimately disregard the industry as a whole. What's more, in parallel, there was a movement by inbound marketing technology vendors against the notion of acquiring new data for use in sales and marketing. There was very little trust among buyers, or brand differentiation between vendors. The belief was that all contact data vendors were the same—unreliable, low quality, and faceless. Even though we offered a range of higher-quality data and service-based offerings, we were grouped into the same category. Game on.

The Solution

We knew we needed to build awareness, get our name in the press, and persuade influencers to talk about us. We had to create buzz. But this strategy had to be about more than *coverage*, it had to position the company as *helpful* in a fast-changing marketing landscape, *innovative* in an industry of subversive practice and, most important, *trustworthy* in a world of unethical vendors.

I started at the company as a marketing manager, but as I took on this endeavor, my title evolved to "Director of Buzz." (Yes, really—I still have the business card years later.) It reflected the importance my team placed on this initiative. This was not just a subset of someone's job, done half-heartedly or part-time.

We started by establishing a holistic plan, one that spanned analyst relations, public relations, events, partnerships, influencers, speaking, awards, and social media. Here are some tenets we followed:

1. Leverage your unique internal assets.

One untapped resource at our disposal was a unique data set of social media profiles associated with our massive database of millions of business contacts and companies. We leveraged this internal data set to uncover trends and create a public-facing narrative about the state of social media use in business (a hot topic at the time and something many organizations were struggling to address). With the help of our internal data science team, we developed the Social Business Report, which analyzed various themes about which job titles, cities, industries, etc., saw the highest use of social media.

These data-driven headlines were compiled into a report format, with accompanying infographics and written analysis. Though the report was ultimately meant to showcase the depths of our data available for customers to purchase, it also drove press and acquired thousands of leads. We hired a PR agency to pitch the trends to relevant publications, and saw coverage in Fox Business, Huffington Post, ZDNet, *Wall Street Journal*, *Washington Post* and industry publications including BtoB Magazine, Mashable, MarketingProfs, and others. I'll never forget how excited our small team was to huddle around a screen watching our CEO interviewed on Fox Business News on the findings of the report. Much scotch was consumed that day.

The findings were repurposed into infographics which were shared heavily on social media and embedded on other industry blogs, since many offered their take on the findings. Their participation drove a sharp increase in traffic back to our site.

We hosted the full report behind a form, driving 18,000 downloads in one year. Questions about the report were posted to us on Twitter and LinkedIn, which we monitored and answered quickly (using our CEO as a company spokesperson). It was an unexpected initiative from a data company like ours, and one that helped us earn air cover while we worked to secure our next round of funding.

2. Be thoughtful about event marketing.

Events and trade shows offer a fantastic opportunity to stand out, when planned for thoughtfully. Because many data vendors in our space operated without much humanity or personality, often hiding behind email and anonymous websites, we knew it was critical to make a strong impression in person with our audience. Events allowed us to do this.

We had some great personalities on our roster who could make a strong connection with customers, and this was critical when selling to enterprise organizations that consumed a large amount of data and services to keep their engines running. At this organization, events ultimately generated the largest-sized deals on average. We directed a large portion of our marketing budget each year to events, and learned a few things along the way:

A. Size isn't everything

Because our larger competitors could afford much larger booths than us, we had to work hard to stand out. Luckily, nobody had given me a rule book when I started. I worked hard to make sure we stood out from the crowd, even in a smaller booth. I employed a variety of tactics, from custom-branded bikes to buttons worn by attendees. One stand-out tactic that fit in a small booth was a branded arcade game filled with rubber ducks and bath loofahs. (We were promoting "clean data" at the time.) The game was set to win 100% of the time via a sneaky panel in the back and it was an absolute hit. Attendees were literally lining up—I am not kidding—to play a free game where they could win a rubber duck. They loved it. And so did my sales team.

B. Nobody wants to "swing by your booth"

Wherever possible, we worked hard to generate meetings and foot traffic to the booth with pre-event promotions. With event sponsorship typically comes a pre-show attendee list. Many vendors sent an email requesting attendees "swing by our booth," but we instead offered something of considerable value in exchange for their time. At some shows, we offered to conduct a free assessment of their data in advance of the show, the results of which we would explore live in-person to offer strategies for improvement and brainstorm solutions. We also selected targeted accounts and offered a copy of the book from that event's keynote speaker, which we had signed, in exchange for a 15-minute live discovery meeting.

This pre-show meeting activity was accompanied by goals—the larger the event, the more meetings we aimed for—and executed in conjunction with our sales development reps who included attendees in their calling plans leading up to the show. They too were incentivized to secure meetings for our reps ahead of the event.

C. A Rising tide lifts all boats

One tactic that worked especially well at events was to maximize the value of partnerships. I always sought to partner with complementary vendors whose combined resources gave us the cash we needed to book space at local hotspots or throw a very exclusive executive dinner event. Our most popular event was a boat party in San Diego that featured hor d'oeuvres, live jazz, and a tour of the harbor. To get on the boat, you needed a ticket from our booth. One of my competitors was so jealous of how popular the event was becoming, and how many leads we earned, they sent their sales team to try to convert attendees to their event by handing out motion sickness pills near our booth.

3. Change the conversation.

Press itself is great, but *meaningful* coverage helps buyers recognize they have a problem they may not be aware of in the first place. You compete with "the way things are done today" before you are ever competing with other vendors in the mind of your prospect. We set out to use our buzz strategy to make prospects aware they had a problem. In essence, we needed to shift the conversation of the industry.

We examined the current narratives in the space, those from our competitors, press, and also the other leading vendors influencing our customers. Our solution offered a differentiating feature that was centered on *quality*. While the rest of the industry spoke of quantity, e.g., how many contacts they offered, we shifted the focus by creating awareness of the business implications of poor data quality.

Our VP of Marketing led the creation of a proprietary research initiative to show how pervasive the issue of quality really was in the market. The results of this report were published as a gated asset, driving thousands of leads, and also giving us excellent coverage in the trade press. What made our asset so interesting to reporters was the simple fact that we were talking about an issue that affected thousands of businesses in a unique new light, backed by statistically sound research. This content was the basis for a range of tactics, including:

- Focused press outreach to generate coverage of the report in business publications
- Fueling blog content for weeks
- The foundation for executive speaking engagements at industry trade shows
- A benchmarking tool for sales to use in consultative selling with prospects
- Bylined articles by our executives in the press spelling out the breadth of this issue and the business impacts
- Infographics that fueled social media activity
- Coverage in industry trade publications and blogs

Though it began as something of a wake-up call for many, the report has been continued year after year, becoming a trusted benchmark for companies to measure against, and consistently positioning our brand as the authority on the state of an industry.

4. Influence those who influence your customers

We knew an important part of breaking through the barrier of mistrust would be to earn the support of the people our customers trusted. We executed an influencer program that created advocates out of those in our space with strong followings. The program had various types of influencers, each treated with special consideration:

- <u>Analysts</u> — Analyst firms require thoughtful relationships with those who cover your space, and it's not always necessary to pay-to-play. Instead, one way to an analyst's heart is to demonstrate your organization's impact on the space they write about through briefings. Share the lessons and trends you're seeing on the front lines, the losses as well as the wins, and always give them ample time ahead of your announcements to know what you're up to. Once you're big enough to afford it, a paid relationship with an analyst firm affords you the opportunity to use their written content in your own marketing efforts. We chose to engage in a paid relationship with only one or two analyst firms who had the most impact on our target audience, but still conducted regular briefings with all firms in the space.

○ <u>Service providers</u> — Many service providers (agencies/brokers/resellers) work to create strong personal brands in the industry, and have the potential to reach many organizations that rely on them to make strategic and tactical recommendations. We knew we had to be in the consideration set of these partners, and ideally among their preferred vendors. We dedicated a full time employee to supporting these partners in their sales and referral efforts, but in marketing, we made sure to promote their successes and champion their brands simultaneously. Whether partner events, co-marketed thought leadership webinars, joint press initiatives and award/speaking proposals, or collaborative content, the public perception of our partners was important to the success of our channel initiative.

○ <u>Who's who</u> — In every industry there is a "who's who" list of what I call celebrities in the space. They're often the ones delivering keynote sessions, racking up thousands of Twitter followers, promoting their recent book, featured in interviews and generally earning a strong army of fans. Maintaining a casual but professional relationship with these celebrities was critical to our success, since the reach of their networks was on par with some industry publications. But these influencers are inundated with requests, just like journalists.

Any relationships we built with celebrities in the space were genuine, fostered on a mutual respect and filled with mutual support. We didn't target just anyone— we made sure there was true relevance and overlap in our target audiences. We made sure our executives had face time with them at industry events, and worked to help them promote their personal brands wherever possible. We would feature their perspective in content initiatives, invite them as guests to executive customer dinners parties, promote their books at our trade show booths, and more. Our efforts ensured that they saw benefit from a relationship with us, and that we earned a place in their public activity where possible exposure to their extensive networks online helped to increase our awareness. Reciprocity matters.

The Results

In one year alone we generated over 90 million online impressions, created over 6,500 qualified leads for sales, and doubled our blog traffic. Our Twitter following grew to 8,000 followers annually (surpassing many of our larger competitors) and we saw steady growth in PR coverage and inbound website traffic. More important, we changed the narrative of the industry and inserted our brand among the conversations that were happening. Much of what we achieved with our buzz strategy was realized downstream with a steady increase in sales.

We hit our stride and maximized brand awareness about four years into my tenure at the organization. Just months later, the company was acquired by Dun and Bradstreet—I'd like to think in part due to the brand equity we were able to create, and the year-over-year growth in both revenue and headcount that resulted from our dedication in this area.

Bzz-bzz.

HOW-TO GUIDELINES: MAKE THE MOST OF YOUR NEXT TRADE SHOW

As an attendee, I hate most trade show booths. Now, *hate* is a strong word, but hear me out. They're often filled with bored salespeople trying to eye my badge to recognize one of their target accounts. Their first question is often "Where are you located?"—not as a polite conversation starter, but rather to discern whether or not I'm in their territory. What's worse, the SWAG (stuff-we-all-get) isn't given much thought. For the record, I need exactly zero more branded pens, stress balls, or T-shirts.

Great event sponsorships are designed as an *experience*. They take into consideration the journey an attendee may have with a brand before the show, during the show, and after the show. It's similar to designing a cohesive customer experience—apply the same thoughtfulness to your next event. Put down the branded squishy ball. Back away from the order form for your next set of logo-adorned beer cozies. Get a whiteboard, and get strategic. It's time to blow your next trade show results out of the water. Here's how:

1. Select the right events.

Event selection is an art and a science, like many other aspects of marketing. Decide to spend your limited resources wisely, taking the following factors into consideration:

a. Location — Consider the costs of travel and executives being out of the office for extended periods of time on cross-country trips. Take into account how many customers or prospects are located in the same region, to maximize your visit.

b. Objectives — Begin with a set of goals and targets for each event, for example what kind of revenue you expect to see from each show. In the past I've used a

3X rule—for the investment I made in each show, I committed to driving 3X that cost in revenue. Consider the following:

- o Size of attendee list — To determine whether this 3X return was feasible, I looked at the overall size of the attendee list, and estimated the percentage who would actually be collected as leads for our team.

- o Typical conversion rates — Our event leads converted at a particular rate, as determined by looking at previous show activity in our CRM. I used these rates to estimate, based on the show's size and number of attendees generally in our target audience, what I could expect to generate from the show.

- o Preference — Every show provides demographic information about its attendees in the sponsor prospectus, but don't be afraid to take this with a grain of salt and do your own research. Understand where your top 10 customers are spending their time.

c. Appeal — Ensure that the event management has a solid plan for attracting the right people (through the right kinds of speakers, compelling musical guest, or other draw).

d. Competitive set — Are your competitors exhibiting at the show? If you're smaller, do some research into where your core competition exhibited in the past that led to their growth. Identify opportunities to stand out, and, if you can't outspend them, do your best to outshine them with a creative event strategy.

e. Your experience — When in doubt, visit the event yourself before investing. Often shows will provide a complimentary ticket to potential sponsors. Ask vendors what they think, and what kinds of results they see. Above all, trust your gut!

2. Start early.

Collect every key deadline months in advance. Understand exactly when you need to ship goods, get your people registered, and figure out when attendees are arriving and leaving. Events are planned months, if not years, in advance to book the right space in a highly competitive calendar. It's like wedding venues—many large shows block off their dates *years* in advance.

Find out when speaking submissions are due. (Hint: it's likely at least six months in advance of the show.) Identify when the big parties and celebrations will be, so you can plan your events around the schedule of the show. Find out when award submissions are due for awards given out at the event, and work with your customers to submit their stories. Plan tactics, plan budget, and you'll be set up for success.

Pre-event meetings are an important part of maximizing your investment and require some foresight. Don't show up and expect your ideal customers to wander down your aisle in the exhibit hall. Book meetings ahead of time with those customers who you know are in town, or who you know are planning to attend the show. Leverage multiple tactics, including email and phone, with an offer than extends beyond "stop by our booth." If meeting with an executive, consider reviewing the results of an assessment. If meeting with an end user, consider training on a new feature. When booking meetings before the show, make your prospect or customer's visit worth their time.

3. Start fresh.

When your trade show booth is half-hearted, your results are subpar. Do you drag the same, tired 8x10 Velcro pop-up banner, brochures, and branded pens to every show? If so, it's time for an intervention. Give that poor pop-up a break. Think about each event as an opportunity to create a memorable experience for your attendees. Humans seek connection, and being in person gives you a fantastic opportunity to create lasting brand equity with them. Especially in this age of digital marketing, facetime has never been so important. Will you be the vendor they remember when they head back to the office? Not with that tired pop-up banner, you won't.

4. Create an overarching theme.

Themes can be inspired by any new products or features you're launching, or by the theme of the show itself and its attendees. Themes should be simple, actionable, and clear. A great theme allows you to select corresponding tactics beneath it, and should be immediately related to your core value proposition. If it requires explanation, it's too complicated. Go back to the drawing board, and don't overthink it.

I recently saw a simple yet effective theme from a tool that helps companies generate more revenue. They homed in on that revenue concept with a cash cow. Literally—a cow filled with money, featured prominently in their booth. The cow appeared on their pre-show emails, landing pages, and direct mail, so it became an easy brand association for attendees by the time they got to the show.

One note of caution: themes can become dangerous if they are selected without a bit of restraint and sanity checking. For example, another data quality services provider attempted to break through the noise at a massive event one year by hiring women to hand out product materials dressed in skimpy French maid outfits. They took the idea of "clean data" to the wrong extreme. I'm sure some men thought it would be a great idea back at the office, but for many female marketing leaders (and sensible male leaders as well) who experienced these women on the sidewalk outside the convention hall, it was trashy, unwelcome, and inappropriate.

5. Get on stage.

Besides creating your well-designed booth and providing thoughtful branded giveaways (which should all align to your overall theme and event experience), your job is to ensure that your brand is *everywhere* at the show. Apply to speak well ahead of the deadline.

Follow these rules to give your session the best possible shot at getting selected:

a. Be original — This goes without saying, but do your best to uncover a *new* way of approaching a common problem facing your customers, address an industry topic with a *fresh* perspective, or present *new* findings or research.

b. Be actionable — Include customer stories and case studies. Provide real tips and tricks. Give actionable takeaways for attendees to use as soon as they leave your session and head back to the office. If possible, get a real customer up on stage with you; attendees will love to hear from their peer (rather than just a vendor) and learn how they solved their problem.

c. Don't be a snowflake — As important as it is to be original in your event topic, look at last year's show agenda, and the year before that. Find out what format and tone works for this event. Each selection committee is different, and will prefer a different style.

d. Be entertaining — Give attendees a reason to come to your session, rather than the three or four scheduled at the same time. If your topic is somewhat dry, tie your title into current events, pop culture references, or use every marketer's secret weapon—puns. Consider different formats such as a game show or tell-all. The rules of what will catch a reader's eye in a blog post title applies to your speaking sessions too. Get creative.

e.   Be credible — The profile of the individual you are putting on stage matters. Work to increase the personal brand of your company spokesperson through a variety of efforts such as authoring a book, winning awards, and other recognition. The more notable your spokesperson, the more event organizers want them on stage.

f.   Be timely — Event selection committees often select speaking slots far in advance to help them sell more tickets to the event. They know attendees decide to spend money on events to hear about the issues facing their business *right now* and in the future. Ensure that your topic is timely based on what's happening in the industry.

6. Get outside the exhibit hall.

Events offer a rare opportunity where your sales teams, executives, and customers are all in the same city. Leverage this opportunity to schedule time outside of the event itself, but remember that you are competing with sessions and packed schedules. To get on the calendar of a busy attendee, you need to offer something compelling. Consider getting four or five of your customers who face similar pain points together over lunch, or take them to an unforgettable experience unique to the city you're in.

Events are expensive. That simple fact alone prevents many organizations from investing in them, opting instead to double down on digital tactics only. While there is no doubt digital marketing affords very clear ROI and massive reach, we are all still selling to living, breathing human beings. These human beings often use as much emotion and intuition as they do logic in making any purchase decision, whether you sell to the CIO or the CMO. Your events are a rare opportunity to forge a human connection—something digital marketing can never truly replicate or replace. To take full advantage of this, plan your next event thoughtfully and with creativity.

CHAPTER 15

Referral Marketing

○ Referred customers have 16% higher customer lifetime value.[33]

○ 73% of executives prefer to work with sales professionals referred by someone they know.[34]

○ 84% of B2B decision makers start the buying process with a referral.[35]

When I launched my consulting practice, it was a true leap of faith into the world of the unknown. I needed to grow my pipeline of projects, and find new opportunities quickly—all without the budget and resources I had throughout my 15 years of in-house marketing positions. What I had was my reputation, experience, and a strong network of people I'd worked with over the years.

I covered the basics of starting a business right away. I formalized the legal entity for my business, bought a web domain and started working on my logo. These were all

---

33 Journal of Marketing, http://knowledge.wharton.upenn.edu/article/turning-social-capital-into-economic-capital-straight-talk-about-word-of-mouth-marketing/

34 Social Buying Meets Social Selling, IDC https://business.linkedin.com/content/dam/business/sales-solutions/global/en_US/c/pdfs/idc-wp-247829.pdf

35 http://smallbiztrends.com/2016/01/b2b-referrals.html

necessary tasks, but none of them would find me my first project. I had enough cash saved to last 90 days without work, when something interesting happened: I secured three projects in 30 days, just by tapping into my network and unlocking referrals in an unexpected way.

As a marketing consultant, I knew that I had to look more polished than the average consultant. Potential clients would care if my logo looked like clip art or my website lacked the basics. So I sent out communication to my network asking them to vote on my new logo. I posted a handful of different options and asked people to vote on what they liked best.

Not only did a clear logo winner emerge, but when people found out I was available for freelance work they looked to see if anything on their to-do list was a good fit. They did this in part to help me, but also because they knew where my skills could add value to their organization.

It was quickly evident to me that I had to tap into one of the most cost-effective and powerful sources of new business: word of mouth and referral marketing. I decided to build my practice 100% on referrals, which meant I had to behave deliberately to reach that goal.

As part of this process, I set certain ground rules toward this objective:

- ❍ **I would only take work where I could excel and provide a measurable impact to the organizations I served.** Whether we sell services, products or some combination, it's tempting to take all work that comes our way. But if building a strong network of ongoing referral business is your goal, it's important that you select work where you can excel and your product or service is a good fit for the needs of the client you hope to serve.

- ❍ **I had to make myself crazy-responsive to all introductions.** Not all introductions are a perfect fit for your business, but you should always aim to show value and make the person who introduced you look good. No matter how busy I am, I make time to take a 15-minute introductory call, refer someone to a relevant article, or introduce them to a peer in my network who can service their needs.

- **I had to be obsessive in my gratitude.** Simply saying thank you is not an option. You must not only say it—you must mean it. When a friend introduced me to her sister company and a project closed, I didn't just buy her a gift card, I bought her a brick oven pizza cookbook and sent a handwritten note, because I knew she'd just built a backyard pizza oven. The personal touch showed my sincerity and was worth the effort.

- **I needed my network to see me as a resource.** Even if they didn't think I could personally be of service, I needed my connections to see me as someone they could ask for guidance and advice. Being asked for recommendations did two things for me: it allowed me to refer my network and help some of them along, and I found a surprising amount of work my network didn't know I'd be available to complete. In fact, 10% of my business each year comes from someone in my network asking me if I know someone that solves a particular problem.

- **I had to be ready with my pitch.** Over the years my practice has evolved, but no matter what, I'm always prepared to answer the question "How can you help us?" When you help others you'd be surprised how many want to reciprocate. That's why it is so important that you have an answer ready when they offer to help you. When they ask, be prepared with something specific. When I'm chatting with an event planner I may respond, "I'm always looking for new speaking opportunities. Are there any events you help coordinate where I might be a good addition to the agenda?"

- **Most of all, I had to stay connected and grow my network consciously every week.** Take note: I didn't ask for work everywhere I went. I wasn't going to get work by sending out a link to the list of services on my website. I got work by publishing research on relevant topics, by doing well on projects, and by making myself available.

My strategy paid off. Below is an example of how an introduction from one person in my network produced work at 14 different companies over a four-year period using the principles above.

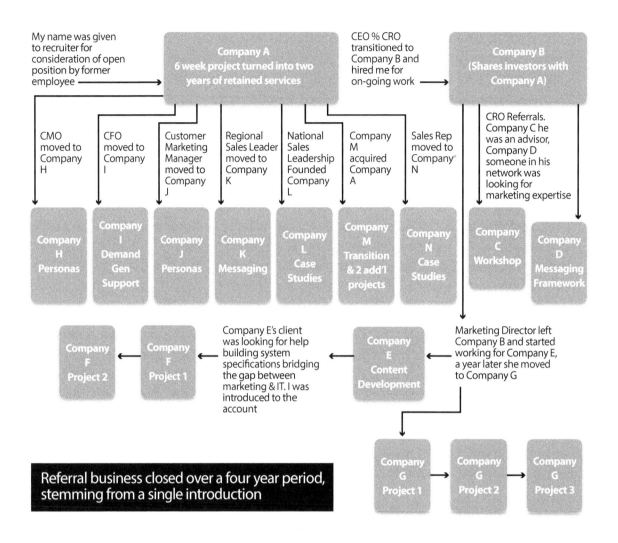

The State of Referral Marketing

Referral strategies are not just relevant for services-oriented or small businesses. Every company, even the largest and most complex organization, is made up of salespeople who work day in and day out to build relationships with buyers. We have support professionals who know customer needs perhaps better than anyone else, plus operations teams and even product development teams that interact with buyers on a daily basis.

How quickly could your business grow if every person on each of these teams was conscious and deliberate about increasing referrals? What kinds of growth would you see if you implemented a true referral strategy?

REFERRAL MARKETING

Most B2B decision makers start the buying process by seeking peer recommendations and referrals, and yet most marketing organizations haven't assigned a single person to own this critical effort. That's right, referrals are one of the most critical pieces of the buyer's journey, yet most businesses don't have any structure around it.

This lack of focus is largely due to the fact that many marketers have a misconception that referrals happen organically as part of other advocate and reference programs. Some do happen naturally, but as marketers we can, and should, facilitate a referral culture by developing a dedicated referral program that has discrete goals, incentives and members. Below, I clarify the difference between these three program types.

Referral programs:

- ○ Can come from any source, not just customers
- ○ Reward revenue, not activity
- ○ Require highly personalized interactions

	Reference Program	Advocate "Influencer" Program	Referral Program
Primary Purpose	Build a library of customers willing to make themselves available for late-stage pipeline opportunity reference checks	Develop a cadre of external evangelists who increase public discussion about a product/service category	Identify active buying opportunities and foster an introduction to those accounts
Common Incentives	○ Renewal discounts ○ Purchase concession (discount if customer agrees to be a reference) ○ Gift cards	○ Vendor swag ○ Gift cards ○ Exclusive event access	○ Gift card (once closed, not based on introduction) ○ Discount available to person being referred ○ Personalized thank-you gift
Primary Contact	○ Sales representative for reference calls ○ PR/Customer Marketing for content deliverables	○ Influencer/advocate marketing	○ Account manager or sales representative

	Reference Program	Advocate "Influencer" Program	Referral Program
Reward Systems	Time Based (the more time requested to perform the activity, the larger the reward)	Volume Based (the more activities undertaken, the bigger the reward. In some cases this is a fee-based relationship (e.g., commissioning a thought leadership paper or a keynote address)	Deal Based (rewards based on value of new business closed)
Vendor Relationship	Customer	Industry experts with a following and credibility	Any
Types of Activities Rewarded	○ Participating in a case study, press release, joint award submission or video testimonial ○ Taking a reference call ○ Speaking at an event hosted by vendor or third party ○ Hosting a site visit	○ Participating in thought leadership content deliverable (e.g., event, article) ○ Posting social content that mentions company ○ Forwarding/sharing communication promoting event or vendor accomplishment	Personal introduction to peer who is likely to need product/service offered

CASE STUDY: OPERATION SHARE THE LOVE

About six weeks before Valentine's Day, my client, an enterprise software company, wanted to accelerate the number of high-conversion opportunities in their pipeline. Their software sold for $15,000 through an inside sales team that was working hard to increase the average revenue per customer by selling new product categories to existing customer organizations.

The Problem

We knew from looking at the conversion data that most leads coming into the company were not sales-ready. Their outbound calling programs, while effective, were anything but efficient. It was costing a lot of time and money to find each new opportunity.

While their sales representatives had solid relationships with customers, they rarely had the opportunity to meet in person and they were always looking for an opportunity to reach out and cement their relationship. In addition, although all their products served related purposes, sometimes the buying trigger would come from a different part of the organization from that which was originally sold. With lofty goals for the quarter looming, this team needed a catalyst to reenergize existing customers and boost opportunities in their pipeline—fast.

The Solution

To increase average revenue per customer and drive toward a lower cost per sale, I knew we could capitalize on an important asset of this company. They had a healthy customer base, most of whom were happy. Building a referral program quickly rose to the top of the to-do list. Without worrying too much about the compressed timeline, we decided Valentine's Day would be the perfect time to launch *Operation Share the Love*.

With less than six weeks to get the program launched we immediately put a plan in place. The program had to meet the following criteria:

1. Be simple to administer
2. Cost less than $4,000 to execute
3. Launch by February 14th (less than six weeks away)

Our initial efforts were quite traditional, but too expensive given the budget constraint. We read through example referral programs, interviewed several customers and outlined point-based reward systems that would earn a wide range of discounts, free training, charitable donations and prizes. Then we did a reality check against the above goals. It turned out that this plan would break the bank, and require a complex point-based workflow that would need to be monitored and explained. Time to reboot.

With time ticking away we built a simple referral program that met our initial criteria, and delivered results. Here's why it worked:

- ○ **It sparked excitement —** We segmented the top 200 clients (defined by revenue) into a physical mailing list. Then we bought giant Hershey's Kisses and did a simple piece of direct mail. Along with the chocolate, we put a tag on the box that proclaimed our love for their organization with a URL to a dedicated "Share the

Love" campaign website. Mailings were sent 7 days before Valentine's Day via regular post. (Note: Be careful when sending chocolate in the mail—temperature variations can alter the texture and quality.)

- **It was friendly** — The remaining customers were sent a friendly email message on Valentine's Day wishing them well and encouraging them to "share the love" as well on our dedicated landing page.

- **Participation was easy** — We knew we had to make it easy for our customers to get involved. The call-to-action was to introduce us to their peers. With a simple click from the landing page, participants were brought to a prefilled email message that opened within their email system. We could track the activity, and the customer could customize the message to make it more personal if they wanted. Other than this, no significant effort was required.

- **We offered incentives** — To encourage participation we offered each program participant a simple motivation: every time they made an introduction, they were entered to win one of three prizes. We gave away a conference pass to a popular industry show, a technical gadget and some company swag. But we also went a step further—we gave participants a time-based discount code that they would be passing along to their peer. That way, they were getting something (a chance to win a prize) but also giving something (a discount code) to their referral.

- **We created urgency** — We made sure to keep the timeframe of the program short to encourage a quick response. Entries to win the prizes and the viability of the discount codes were only valid for the next five weeks.

- **We covered the logistics** — It's challenging enough to execute a great program, but where many companies fall short is communicating thoughtfully to the right clients. We made contest rules easy to find, suppressed clients from the mailing who had outstanding support issues, and worked with sales to map out how we would treat the referral introductions.

The Results

Just 18 hours after launch we saw 20 introductions and a demo request. My client was thrilled, and their sales team was feeling the love. Over the next three weeks, an additional 22 introductions were made within customer organizations and five new deals entered the pipeline.

Operation Share the Love was a point-in-time program but it did more than generate five new opportunities—it was the first step in creating a referral culture at this organization.

HOW-TO GUIDELINES: BUILD A SCALABLE REFERRAL CULTURE

While some individuals on your sales team may be naturally good at seeking referrals, by developing a formal structure you'll gain significant scale and predictability.

When building your program consider these elements:

○ **Seek both external and internal referrals.** When we consider seeking referrals we often expect our customer contacts to introduce us to another organization. However, we should not forget that recommending our product or service to a peer from a different business unit or division at their own company is just as valuable (and often easier) for your contact to do.

○ **Make it easy for your team to show their gratitude.** Don't automate the thank-you process—the power of a handwritten note is extraordinary. However, you can make it easy for your team to show their gratitude by having cards readily available, along with gifts and company swag. Where possible, encourage your team to use gifts that are of personal sentiment and make it easy for them to expense an item you might not have in inventory. Keep in mind, these are gestures of appreciation and should never be perceived as paying for the referral. A good rule of thumb is to keep the value under $50 and take note of contacts who cannot accept anything of monetary value. Consider charitable donations to a cause they care about as an alternative for individuals who cannot accept gifts.

○ **Consider employee incentives.** Your sales team has a natural incentive, a commission, for seeking referrals, but for the rest of the company, referrals aren't as top-of-mind. All employees have the potential to generate referrals, and many who serve customers are in fact in a better position than sales to ask for them. Make referrals a recognized part of the customer satisfaction and advocacy initiative internally, and unleash this hidden asset. You may even want to conduct an employee referral contest with prizes.

○ **Find the right times to trigger conversations.** There are many customer interactions that can be used to trigger communication, and you typically want to capitalize on the positive moments. For example, when your product goes live for the first time, encourage your champion to send out a companywide announcement spreading the good news to other parts of the operation. Other opportunities arise when a positive review is published, or you received a strong rating after a support call. These are all excellent times to initiate dialogue, say thank you, and request a referral.

- ○ **Make it easy to refer.** Don't forget to pay attention to how referrals are made. Make it easy for the person making the referral to know who they should introduce and where they can find information to share about your product or service. Also, make sure the person receiving the referral is well prepared to respond quickly.

- ○ **Automate nurture streams.** As marketers, we often focus on building a nurture stream for new buyers we want to help along on the buyer's journey, but it's equally important to build content streams for those who are not buyers, but potential referral sources. The good news is, you can reuse content in other channels, but the context within which it is delivered and the frequency of communications will be different.

  When nurturing referral sources, remember:

  - ○ **Cadence.** Use a less frequent cadence than you would for potential opportunities with your email communication—no more than once a month. This is a good way to leverage newsletters.

  - ○ **Channels.** Keep the dialogue going via social channels. Not only should you post communications on your social channels, but, more important, you should be responding to, commenting on and sharing their content.

  - ○ **Content.** Communications should be heavy on industry research and case studies—content that your referral source can use to foster an introduction and position you as an expert.

  - ○ **Promotions.** Consider special promotions to incent referrals that you can use sparingly, 2–3 times a year.

The power of referral marketing is well within reach with some creativity and structured thinking. It should be noted that the foundation of any successful referral initiative, whether a point-in-time campaign or a sustained referral culture, is happy customers who have a positive experience with your buying process and offering. Our most critical imperative is to delight customers, not only for successful referrals, but as a sustained competitive advantage.

CONCLUSION

Using Unleash Possible To Effect Change

In the introduction I told you I was sharing my lessons learned and best practices because there wasn't a single thing in the entire book that you can't do. It's not about how much money you have, or how big or small your team has become. Unleashing what's possible is about committing to what's critical and measuring what matters.

Unleash Possible can help you decide how to apply your passion and how to attract not just more buyers, but the right ones. You are now ready to start applying what you've learned. I've outlined a few next steps to get you started.

- ○ Use the referenced templates to start documenting next steps. Complimentary copies can be found at www.unleashpossible.com/templates

- ○ Host a lunch-and-learn. Pick one chapter that resonated most with you and share a summary of the lessons learned with your team. Using the techniques from Chapter 1, brainstorm opportunities to apply the chapter's principles to your own business.

- ○ Start a book club. Encourage colleagues from across the business to read *Unleash Possible* and host three book club meetings, one for each section of the book. During the meetings look for ways to apply what the team has learned within your organization.

While I have attempted to break down complex concepts into actionable steps, I recognize there is a *lot* to digest. If you have questions, need clarification or simply want to share how you've applied these ideas to your business, please reach out. You can find me at @samanthastone on Twitter or via email at samantha.stone@marketingadvisorynetwork.com.

CPSIA information can be obtained
at www.ICGtesting.com
Printed in the USA
LVHW101113131118
596628LV00020B/45/P